Teaching with AI

Teaching with AI

A PRACTICAL GUIDE TO A NEW ERA OF HUMAN LEARNING

José Antonio Bowen
and C. Edward Watson

Published in association with the American Association of Colleges and Universities

AAC&U

JOHNS HOPKINS UNIVERSITY PRESS
Baltimore

Printed in the United States of America on acid-free paper
2 4 6 8 9 7 5 3 1

Johns Hopkins University Press
2715 North Charles Street
Baltimore, Maryland 21218
www.press.jhu.edu

Cataloging-in-Publication data is available from the Library of Congress
A catalog record for this book is available from the British Library.

ISBN: 978-1-4214-4922-7 (paperback)
ISBN: 978-1-4214-4923-4 (ebook)

CONTENTS

CHRONOLOGY

1950s Artificial intelligence research gets going but is focused on expert or logical systems.

1959 Arthur Samuel coins the term "machine learning"

1967 Joseph Weizenbaum creates Eliza, the first significant chatbot and LLM that marked the beginning of work into natural language processing (NLP).

1980s Google's search algorithm, which learns from your search history, helps stir a revival in machine learning as an AI strategy.

1990s Deep Learning and Artificial Neural Network research begins to grow.

1997 IBM's DeepBlue beats Garry Kasparov in chess.

2010 DeepMind founded by Demis Hassabis, Shane Legg, and Mustafa Suleyman.

2014 Ian Goodfellow proposes Generative Adversarial Networks, which lead to many new types of neural networks that are both generative and able to be trained.

2016 AlphaGo (a machine learning AI from DeepMind) beats world champion Lee Sedol at Go.

2017 Transformers makes it possible to both decode and generate new text.

2018 First GPT LLM created by OpenAI.

2021 DALL-E, built on GPT-3, is a machine learning model that generates images.

2022 GPT-3.5 launched in November; AI apps begin to proliferate.

2023 GPT-4 released in March, followed by Bard (by Google), Claude (by Anthropic), LLaMA (by Meta) and Grok (by X).

Introduction

Nothing in life is to be feared, it is only to be understood.
Now is the time to understand more, so that we may fear less.

MARIE CURIE, Nobel Laureate in Physics (1903)
and Chemistry (1911)

There is a great deal to understand about AI. Like the internet, AI is a technology that is going to change everything—and not just education.

The internet, and more specifically, the World Wide Web, fundamentally changed our relationship with knowledge: moving us from a world where knowledge was scarce (but mostly reliable) to one where knowledge was abundant (but largely unreliable). When this framing was first floated (Bowen, 2006), we were all using the internet on our desktops: the iPhone was yet to arrive. We could all appreciate the increased access to research materials and expertise, but we were already wary of the rise of unfiltered and sometimes sinister misinformation. And with the struggles of dial-up, it was easy to underestimate the coming ubiquity of the new technology. Speed, ease of access,

and platforms changed the mechanics and magnified the effect, but not the trajectory. Our relationship with knowledge was changed forever, and in turn everything from education and shopping to culture and politics were altered.

If the internet changed our relationship with knowledge, AI is going to change our relationship with thinking. It is already challenging ideas about creativity and originality, and it will forever alter education, work, and even how we think about thinking (both human and AI "thinking").

Perhaps we can learn some lessons from the rise of the internet. Just as later technologies (like the iPhone and social media) amplified the effects of the internet, we can assume that AI is going to get better and more intertwined with our lives in the future. Banning web-based tools like Wikipedia failed, but would the internet have turned out differently if we had put different constraints on how it developed?

AI has already challenged and divided us faster than the internet did. Some of what we present will have evolved by the time this gets to publication. Still, in 2006, we didn't need to know the specific convergence devices or social media platforms that were to come to know that information would soon be less reliable. Rapid change is again unfolding, and we can use what AI can already do to plan for a future in which our relationship with thinking will be fundamentally altered.

Ethics and Equity

We have tried to keep this book short and focused on the practical. On almost every page, we could have, and maybe should have, dived into ethical problems and ambiguities. We are sure someone will write that book.

As we learned from the internet and social media, there are a million ways the expansion of AI could go wrong and increase inequities, take jobs, and damage human lives. But if you watch Netflix, use a spam filter, shop at Amazon, or drive a car, you are already a part of the new AI economy. The creation of consumer-grade, much more human-sounding chatbots has brought attention to AI and is a real breakthrough that will change our lives. The implications of being able to process virtually anything (data, music, images, computer code, DNA, or brain waves) as language and at scale, however, is mind-blowing and needs careful consideration. It is essential that educators start to talk about these issues with students; if we want students to use AI responsibly, both in school and beyond, AI ethics must be baked into curriculum and include AI literacy, an emerging essential skill.

AI is already increasing inequity both in education and beyond, but it also has the potential to be a tool for equity: AI can provide more feedback to improve learning, increase human creativity, and customize materials for groups or individual students. Teachers will be in an important position to determine whether AI transforms education for better or worse. We tried to provide multiple examples of this with the goal of offering the most practical and urgent information.

You won't like every suggestion or application of AI, but we avoided too much commentary to keep the book from becoming a brick. We have left space for you to make up your own mind.

Students

We quote as much data on how students are using AI as we could find, but given the speed at which things are changing, we also

did our own research. We talked to a lot of students, mostly in small groups. We interviewed students from many different types of institutions: public and private, elite, and regional, two-year colleges to R1 doctoral universities. We also asked students to read key sections and chapters (especially on cheating). It was not a large statistical sample, but we used this feedback and these personal stories to add context to the larger research findings.

Your students may be different, but we urge you to consider that students do not like admitting to cheating or what might be viewed as questionable or embarrassing practices to their own faculty (or to their parents or to researchers). In the same way that voters often say one thing in a survey and then do another in the ballot box, the students we interviewed consistently reported that everyone, 100%, of students were using AI. This is not a finding replicated in surveys, but the questions in those surveys vary. Students were quick to point out that there were lots of different types of usage, and that they did not consider a lot of it to be cheating.

Outline and Organization

This book is organized into three parts: thinking with AI, teaching with AI, and learning with AI.

The first part is about how AI works and what it is doing to the human experience. Chapter 1 starts with terms and enough history to illuminate why this all seems so sudden. If you really don't care what GPT stands for and why it matters, you can skip this bit. (The really important implications appear in chapters 2, 3, and 4.) And yes, the CS experts we asked to read chapter 1

questioned some of our colorful analogies in the drafts, so apologies for this more technical chapter.

Do not skip chapter 2, which chronicles how the world of work (and job interviews!) has already changed for our graduates: AI will eliminate some jobs, but it seems very likely to change every job. This could be good or bad, but we are all likely to be asked to do more and better work more quickly.

AI literacy requires knowing enough about how AI works to be able to use it effectively. Breaking down problems and asking better questions have long been a cornerstone of higher education, and these are critical skills in using AI too. Chapter 3 categorizes this process—from articulating the problem, finding the right AI for the task, creating better prompts, and then iterating with AI. Chapter 4 focuses especially on the uniquely creative nature of AI: as a prediction machine without the inhibitions of social embarrassment, an AI will say anything. The problem of "hallucinating" becomes a strength when the task is coming up with new ideas. In both chapters, it becomes clear that the benefits that come from AI, come from using it as a partner to human thinking.

Part II shifts the focus to teaching. Chapter 5 looks at what AI can already do for faculty and what it might soon do. Chapter 6 analyzes the much-discussed problem of cheating, with research-backed findings about AI detection, which is functionally more challenging than plagiarism detection. Understanding cheating is essential not because detectors will eliminate it, but so we can redesign assignments that will make cheating less rewarding and useful while also improving learning. If students are collaborating with AI to produce better work, they may be on to something. What we call cheating, businesses see as innovation.

From this, follows a discussion of potential policies (chapter 7) and grading (chapter 8). Since all assignments are now AI assignments, you need a policy that defines how work should be done and why. Grading especially needs to be rethought: no one is going to hire a student who can only do C work if an AI can do it more cheaply. We will need to define what "better than AI" work looks like.

The last part of the book is devoted to designing assessments and assignments in this new era. Chapter 9 looks at how AI can customize learning and create individual feedback for students. Chapter 10 outlines new design principles and how we can better guide process and make it visible. The last two chapters apply these principles in copious examples, with chapter 11 focusing on writing and chapter 12 experimenting with new ideas.

Prompts and Responses

We obviously spent a lot of time testing ideas with different AIs. We list many of our specific prompts identified with a gray bar on the left. We wanted it to be very clear when we were quoting exactly from an AI, so we've listed AI responses italics, with a gray bar on the right. We've also listed the AI we used, the version, and the date (APA currently only suggests the date, but the version, GPT-3.5, 4 or Turbo, for example, also matters). AIs tend to be verbose, so most of the responses are abridged (which is also indicated).

We reran prompts as close to the publication date as possible, often with newer versions of a particular AI. Sometimes, we left an earlier response or used the free GPT 3.5 response to show what a cheap and basic response might be. Sometimes

good is good enough, and we know that many students and faculty will be limited to free versions. Since prompts will return a different and unique answer each time, we have included responses only where they were important to the point at hand: showing complete responses from multiple AIs would have made this book much longer for limited gain. You will want to customize and experiment with the prompts yourself.

PART I

Thinking with AI

CHAPTER 1

AI Basics

> AI is one of the most important things humanity is working on. It is more profound than electricity or fire.
>
> **SUNDAR PICHAI,** CEO of Google and Alphabet

If you were busy on November 30, 2022, you might have missed the early demo that OpenAI released of its new chatbot. But after five days, more than a million people had tried it. It reached 100 million daily active users in two months. It took TikTok nine months and Instagram two and a half years to reach that milestone (Hu, 2023).

But bigger than fire? Sundar Pichai has made this comparison repeatedly, but few of us were listening when he said it publicly in January 2016 (when he also admitted he did not really know how AI worked). Fire, like other human technological achievements, has been a double-edged sword; a source of destruction and change as well as an accelerant to advancements. AI is already on a similar trajectory.

Most of us have heard of AI; some may even remember when a computer beat the chess world champion, but that was a

different sort of AI. As happens in many fields (think mRNA vaccines), research over decades takes a turn or finds a new application, and a technology that has been evolving over years suddenly bursts into public awareness.

For centuries, humans looked for easy ways to rekindle fire in the middle of the night. Early chemical versions from Robert Boyle (in the 1680s) to Jean Chancel (1805) were expensive, dangerous, or both and never made it to mass production. Then, chemist John Walker accidentally discovered (in 1826) that friction could make the process safe and cheap. Like matches, seventy years of scholarly work in AI helped create the recent explosion of awareness , but in a GPT flicker, the world has changed.

Expert Systems vs. Machine Learning

The term **artificial intelligence** (AI) was coined in 1956 at a conference sponsored by the Defense Advanced Research Projects Agency (DARPA) to imagine, study, and create machines capable of performing tasks that typically require human cognition and intelligence. (We've highlighted key terms when they are first defined and summarized them in the sidebar glossaries.)

Early AI research focused on logic or **expert systems** that used rules designed to anticipate a wide range of possible scenarios. These systems don't improve with more iterations. This is how robots and AI are still often portrayed in stories. Even in *Star Trek*, the Emergency Medical Hologram is constantly limited by his programming.

IBM pioneer Arthur Samuel (1959) coined the term **machine learning** to describe statistical algorithms that could general-

ize and "learn to play a better game of checkers than can be played by the person who wrote the program." For a simple game like checkers, it was possible to develop an expert system that could search a database but also make inferences beyond existing solutions. Samuel's checkers program, however, was "given only the rules of the game, a sense of direction, and a redundant and incomplete list of parameters which are thought to have something to do with the game, but whose correct signs and relative weights are unknown and unspecified" (Samuel, 1959).

Expert systems (and their logical reasoning) initially dominated research, but machine learning (with its probabilistic reasoning) was more useful in recognizing patterns; it became a more central part of AI research in the 1990s (Langley, 2011). With more memory and larger datasets, statistical algorithms were able to deduce medical diagnoses (WebMD, for example) and eventually led to IBM's Deep Blue chess program beating chess champion Garry Kasparov in 1997.

Machine Learning + Neural Networks = Foundational Models

Neural networks are computing systems modeled like the neural connections in the human brain. Neural networks are a specific type of machine learning model where **nodes** (individual computational units) are organized into layers that mirror our understanding of the human brain. In the 1960s and '70s, networks were logical and linear if-then structures (like following directions from your GPS), but they have become more decentralized layers of interconnected nodes (like knowing lots of different ways to get between two points).

Neural networks need to be trained, usually on large datasets. This training can be either "**supervised**," where the data is labeled so that the model learns the associations between inputs and desired outputs, or "**unsupervised**," where the input data is unlabeled. Once a supervised model is trained, it can classify new inputs: this is how your spam filter works. Unsupervised machine learning generally requires larger datasets but can then associate or cluster unseen trends and relationships: the more you watch Netflix, the more it discovers connections among the things you actually like (and realizes that the documentary you saved about goldfish was a mistake).

A third machine learning paradigm (alongside supervised and unsupervised) is **reinforcement learning (RL)**. Here, neural networks are fed often smaller amounts of unlabeled data but allow the algorithm to interact in an environment where specific outputs are rewarded: when you click on Facebook ads, you are more likely to see those ads again.

Deep learning (DL) is a related training technique where "deep" refers to the multiple layers of the network needed to transform data; simpler tasks reside deeper in the network and then combine to inform output layers. In facial recognition, for example, the model needs first to recognize which groups of pixels constitute faces before it can extract features and then finally match features to known faces.

These machine learning techniques mirror human learning with both its advantages and disadvantages. London-based DeepMind, now a subsidiary of Google, could have taught its Deep Q-Network to play video games like Pong by programming in the rules (an expert systems approach). This (like cheating)

would have been faster, but by using these much slower trial-and-error techniques, Deep Q-Network could now generalize and, like humans, learn the next Atari game much faster. Since the model was learning directly from data, it could also create strategy in ways not limited by human assumptions (with implications for both creativity, [see chapter 4], and accuracy [see below]). These DeepMind programs took longer to learn for themselves, but eventually exceeded human capabilities (Mnih et al., 2015).

Together, deep neural networks and machine learning techniques allow us to build **foundational models.** Since they are trained on very large and varied datasets, they are general-purpose systems whose broad capabilities are still being discovered: few anticipated that these new models could decode brain scans (fMRI) back into the images that subjects were viewing (Chen, 2022; Takagi & Nishimoto, 2023). Part of what makes new AI technology so different, and potentially dangerous, is that we are still discovering what it can do.

Large Language Models (LLMs) are foundational models that were initially focused on language but also created new ways to analyze DNA, music, computer code, and brain waves. The big six LLMs we have today: are GPT (from OpenAI), PaLM (from Google), LLaMA (from Meta), Claude (from Anthropic), Pi (from Inflection), Grok (from xAI). See figure 1.1.

Think of these models as different types of intelligence (like comparing Marie Curie, Maya Angelou, and Cesar Chavez). They are different in neural networks, and they have been trained differently: different (metaphorically) in both nature and nurture.

Glossary I

Artificial Intelligence (AI) refers to the ability of computer systems to mimic human intelligence and also to the development of such systems.

Expert Systems use rules and logic to anticipate a wide range of possible scenarios.

Machine Learning uses probability and statistics to recognize patterns and generalize.

Neural Networks are computing systems modeled like the neural connections in the human brain.

Foundational Models are deep neural networks trained with a large data set using machine learning techniques that mimic human trial and error.

Large Language Models (LLMs) are foundational models focused on language.

GPT stands for Generative Pre-trained Transformers. Foundational models and LLMs all use GPT architecture; it is not unique to OpenAI or ChatGPT.

Diffusion Models are a type of foundational model used to create images and video. Tools like DALL-E, Stable Diffusion, Midjourney are trained by adding noise to the training data which the model learns to remove.

The Turing Test and AI Thinking

Alan Turing first considered the question "Can machines think?" in his paper "Computing Machinery and Intelligence" (Turing, 1950). Turing argued that since "thinking" is hard to define, his original question is meaningless, and he replaced it with a version of the "imitation game" where the interrogator asks two

players questions and receives answers, all through text on computer screens. In Turing's twist, one subject is a human and the other is an AI; the interrogator attempts to determine which is the human. What we now call the "Turing Test" is *not* about thinking, consciousness, intelligence, understanding, sentience, or anything to do with *how* a program might be processing. It is Turing's replacement of the question "Can machines think?" with the question "Can this chatbot make us believe we are interacting with a human?"

In 2022, Google engineer Blake Lemione was fired for claiming that Google's chatbot had become sentient (Grant & Metz, 2022): a clear pass of the Turing Test. An AI does not have to think: *believing* a chatbot is sentient is enough.

LLMs use a combination of technologies to mimic human language and predict the next word, including deep neural networks that mimic human learning, increasing computer speed and capacity, vast amounts of existing human data, and a renewed emphasis on a machine learning strategy that relies on probability and statistics. In the same way that adding friction to a match creates fire in a new way, the returning focus on probability and machine learning in the 1990s unlocked the door to new generative AI. After encountering GPT-3 in 2020, philosopher David Chalmers wrote "it suggests a potential mindless path to **artificial general intelligence** (or AGI)" (Chalmers, 2020). ChatGPT was a breakthrough, but it was also built on compromises.

Hallucinations and Bias: The *G* and the *P* in GPT

The process of pre-training (the *P* in Generative Pre-trained Transformers or GPT models) an AI is lengthy and requires an

enormous dataset (GPT-3 was trained on 45 terabytes of textual data; more than 12 trillion words). That is also why Large Language Models are "large." Since the pretraining sources (including the monthly Common Crawl dataset taken from billions of web pages) contains the good, bad, and ugly of human thought, and since LLMs assimilate to predict, they are bound to reproduce the bias and hate in their source material.

AI can also *amplify* the bias on the internet. When Stable Diffusion, an AI capable of creating photorealistic images, is asked to create images related to high-paying jobs, the images have lighter skin tones than when asked about lower-paying jobs, with three times as many men over women in the high-paying jobs. When asked for images of "doctors," only 7% of the images generated are women, when 39% of US doctors are women: Stable Diffusion exaggerates existing inequities, which is apparent in images in the internet training set (Nicoletti & Bass, 2023). Images generated by other AI image creators also yield biases.

Adobe's Firefly AI image generator tries to correct this by making the number of women or Black doctors proportional to the population of that group in the United States: half the images of doctors it generates are women, and 14% of the doctors are Black, even though only 6% of US doctors are Black (Howard, 2023). Firefly has been trained to increase the probability that a request for an image of a Supreme Court justice in 1960 will be a woman, even though Sandra Day O'Connor became the first woman appointed to the Court in 1981.

Bias can come from training data, but the well-intentioned Firefly examples highlight another set of potential problems: human reviewers who rate and provide feedback for the models output also have bias. If AIs can create images of the world

as it could be or as it is, who gets to choose? Bias can also be hidden in network architecture, decoding algorithms, model goals, and perhaps more worrisome, in the undiscovered potential of these models.

The *G* in GPT is for "generative." Because these models "generate" new sentences, images, and ideas by sorting probabilities of a next word or pixel, they are prone to "generate" false data or "fabricate" fictional references. This ability to "hallucinate" makes AI a terrific tool for creativity: it will put ideas and words together in ways that humans might never have done before (more on this in chapter 4). This same design feature that allows LLMs to provide new and different answers to the same prompt, also causes unpredictability and a lack of reliability. AI is also generative of misinformation.

There are ways to reduce both of these problems, but they will be difficult to eliminate because both are direct consequences of the ways AIs learn to mimic human thinking. The bias is largely a result of the "Pre-training", and the potential for "hallucination" is built into the "Generative" part of GPT.

Transformers: The *T* in GPT

Understanding the *T* in GPT (transformers, but not the one in the movies) is harder and also puts "parameters" and "tokens" in our path.

Every internal variable in a neural network that can be tuned or adjusted to change the output is a **parameter**. A simple parameter is the number of possible words that might go next in a sentence. A hyperparameter is a configuration of variables like the randomness, creativity, or "temperature" of which response is chosen. When the temperature is set to 0, the model

is at its most deterministic: it will return the next word with the highest probability. At higher temperatures, less probable words can be chosen, which leads to more creativity and diversity, but also more potential nonsense and hallucination. The Bing/Copilot conversational style buttons—creative, balanced, or precise—seem to regulate temperature. A model is trained by feeding it examples and tuning its parameters to adjust the output.

GPT-2 had 1.5 billion parameters, GPT-3 had 175 billion parameters, and GPT-4 was estimated to have 1.76 trillion parameters and significantly more memory (Griffith, 2023; Geyer, 2023). More parameters allow for more choices and nuance, so GPT-4 is smarter, more factual, more multilingual, and multimodal (able to accept visual or audio prompts). GPT-4 can create graphs or use an image of what is in your refrigerator to generate recipe ideas. But more parameters can also be slower and more costly. For some tasks, GPT-3.5 is good enough or even better, but while GPT-3.5 failed the bar exam, GPT-4 immediately passed, doing better than most humans (Katz et al., 2023). Professor Anna Mills was a beta-tester and quickly noticed that GPT-4 wrote more sophisticated, precise, articulate, and connected prose, with more varied sentence structure, word choice, information, and examples than GPT-3.5 (Mills, 2023b). All of those extra parameters allow users to imitate your professor or write like Yoda.

A neural network deals only with numbers, so words (or images or brain waves) need to be turned into **tokens,** which are a kind of digital stand-in. Tokens are a series of 0s and 1s that represent words, parts of a word, or other data. More tokens imply more vocabulary, context, and nuance, but both the process of turning words into numbers ("tokenization") and size matter.

Claude (100,000 tokens or 75,000 words) and GPT-4 Turbo (128,000 tokens or 96,000 words) can both read your novel all at once. GPT-4 can also tokenize and analyze images, which Claude cannot.

An AI determines the meaning of a token by observing it in context—what other tokens (words or images) appear near it and how often. Initially, each word in a sequence was processed sequentially. The 2017 breakthrough of **transformers** (the *T* you've been waiting for) provided every token with a weight that internalized the context of the token compared with any other token (Uszkoreit, 2017; Vaswani et al., 2017). This "self-attention" allowed each word to be processed simultaneously, which greatly increased speed and created a more "natural" way to embed context. Transformers allow an AI to look not just at the probability of the next token, but at multiple combinations of tokens and larger patterns at once. Transformers opened the door for human-sounding LLMs but also unified the many disparate disciplines of AI into one of a field where everything—from images, code, music, or DNA—can be treated like language. This synchronicity (which echoes the predictions of a coming convergence or singularity) is one of the reasons why LLMs have become the central foundation models and why change has appeared to occur so quickly. Public access to a functioning GPT on November 30, 2022, also helped shape that perception.

Glossary II

Natural Language Processing (NLP) is a field of AI and linguistics that aims to enable machines to understand, interpret

and create human language. They are essential for search engines and analyzing your social media content. LLMs use NLP to train deep neural networks but LLMs are also used in NLP applications.

Parameters are internal variables in a neural network that can be tuned or adjusted to change the output.

Tokens are the representations of words, parts of words, characters, or punctuation in code and are a focus of NLP.

Transformers (or **"self-attention"**) provide every token with a weight that allows tokens to be compared to any other token simultaneously.

An **Application Programming Interface (API)** is a set of tools for building software applications that can interact with a foundation model. Most of the AI tools and products we are using are not LLMs themselves but are powered by underlying LLMs.

Fine-tuning is the process of customizing pre-trained foundational models (using an API) to do specific tasks. There is an ambiguity here, but for most people it is probably close enough to think of ChatGPT as fine-tuned or powered by GPT, and not its own LLM (Google's Bard has a similar relationship to Gemini).

Generative Artificial Intelligence (GAI) is any type of AI that uses deep learning models to generate or create new content. LLMs and Diffusion Models are both examples of GAI.

Artificial General Intelligence (AGI) is the computer science holy grail that someday an AI will be able to think, make decisions and even feel like humans can. It's basically a person.

Tools and Trade-offs

The established, publicly accessible LLMs you know all use Generative Pre-Trained Transformers (GPT), but they are not all the same:

- Claude 2 (released by Anthropic on July 11, 2023) seems obsessively focused on safety and making AI obey human values (Rose, 2023). With fewer parameters (860 million), Claude is significantly leaner and faster than GPT-4. But Claude is built with many more tokens. This gives Claude a deeper understanding of context and makes its answers more readable and even poetic and (so far) more likely to avoid AI detection tools (Hines, 2023; Rose, 2023). Reviews also find that Claude 2 is better able to solve complex math problems (showing step-by-step work) and to give precise legal analysis (Garst, 2023).
- Grok moves in the other direction with fewer safety guardrails and will answer more questions with more humor and sarcasm. Real-time information from X (formerly Twitter) could be an advantage for staying current, but Grok has only 8,192 tokens and 33 billion parameters and has been subject to less testing and training. It is also limited to a premium (fee) service.
- The free ChatGPT 3-5 is not connected to the internet. And if you ask it a specific question about something recent, it is likely to create fictional references. GPT 4 is a substantially smarter and better AI; do not assume you understand anything about AI until you have used it for several hours.

- Microsoft is heavily invested in OpenAI, so Bing/Copilot Chat gives you a free way to try GPT 4/Turbo. Precise mode is the best way to search for accurate information from the internet.
- Google has its own AI, Bard (with a similar 1.6 trillion parameters), that allows you to click on highlighted statements or click the "Google button" that allows you to check the veracity of information against a web search.
- LLaMA 2 is Meta's family of open source LLMs, so you can download an LLM and build your own AI tool. HuggingChat (from Hugging Face) is an application that uses LLaMA; importantly, it is free with no registration required.
- Pi is designed to be a conversational personal assistant. Pi is chatty, but not connected to the internet, so it works well for practice or learning conversations (described in chapter 9).

Foundational models can be further fine-tuned for specific tasks. Perplexity is optimized for internet searches (using GPT 3.5 or 4 for a fee), and Poe gives you access to multiple AIs at once. What AI tool you should use depends on what you want to accomplish: Do you want speed, reliability, or access to the internet? Do you want to upload images or extra text from video?

When the iPhone connected the internet to the phone, we soon realized that we didn't need information about every flight leaving every day; we just needed to know whether our flight today was delayed. An airline app is better for that task. Apps

were created to focus on making specific tasks easier and faster. Like the apps on your phone, specialized and often fine-tuned apps using APIs will focus your interaction with base models. Indeed, the new OpenAI store is modeled on the Apple App Store and sells customized "GPTs." You can also fine-tune your own application from the pre-trained LLaMA family.

One group of tools (Elicit, Consensus, and ResearchRabbit) connects ChatGPT with Semantic Scholar's database of 175 million papers to make literature searches significantly faster and reliable. Other research tools (like Quivr, Jenni, and ExplainPaper) connect to the internet to verify information. (More about specific tools in chapters 5 and 6.)

The top line of figure 1.1 shows the current big six LLMs (from Google, X, OpenAI, Anthropic, Inflection and Meta: expect Apple and Amazon to join). Below them are an array of API

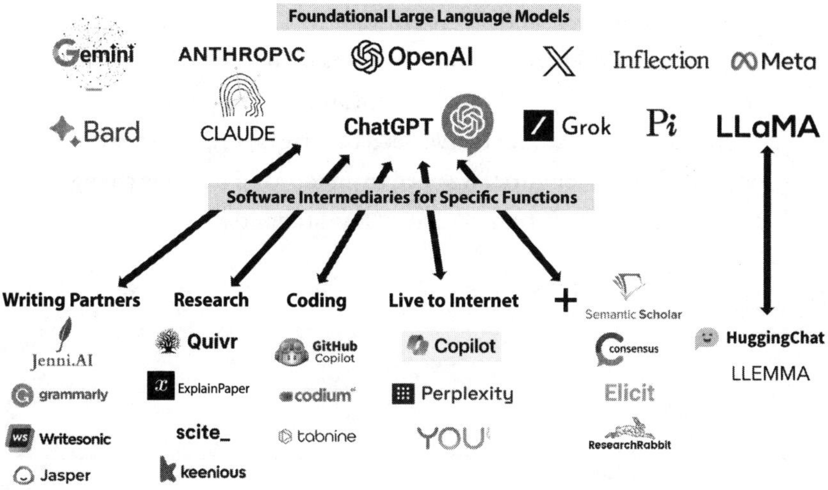

Figure 1.1 The top line shows different Foundational LLMs with some of the software "apps" that interface with them through APIs.

tools. Most of these interact with ChatGPT since it was the first to market, but that will change over time. Microsoft and Google are integrating their Bing/Copilot and Bard AIs directly into their other products, and you can add extensions to summarize YouTube videos or plan a vacation on Expedia. The reality is that you won't be able to keep track of all of the AI lurking in your life (and don't even think about what insurance companies, advertisers, or the government could do with the data your car knows about you), but as with phone apps, it will be useful to know about the variety of AIs on the market and which specific tasks each can perform for you (and which does a task better than another).

AI is not new: it has been curating your social media feed and recommendations for years. This publicly emerging new wave of AI, however, is different. Previous AI helped *curate* your world (or what you saw and read online), but GPT AI will allow you to *create* your world. We are only beginning to learn what AI can do, but AI literacy will be an essential work- and life-skill for both faculty and students. We need to integrate AI-literacy into our classrooms, but first, we need to understand how it is changing work and the future careers of our students.

CHAPTER 2

A New Era of Work

See the patient, not the technology.

AUGMEDIX TAGLINE

Generative AI is a different technology, and the way it is changing work is different too. While previous technological revolutions targeted the skilled but often manual jobs of factory workers, telephone operators, travel agents, and farmers, AI appears set to be more disruptive to lawyers, doctors, copywriters, insurance underwriters, translators, artists, and anyone who works with text. Initial predictions suggest that AI may have little effect in construction (6% of current work tasks) or building and grounds maintenance (1%) but much higher effects in business and financial operations (35%), science (36%), engineering (37%), legal (44%), and administrative support (46%) (Briggs & Kodnani, 2023). Vast new efficiencies are being discovered across a wide range of white-collar sectors, and the expectation is that the impact will be akin to the industrial revolution where a single individual will accomplish work that previously required a team (Bannon, 2023).

This will be a different type of revolution—not because it eliminates a few categories of work, but because it will change the nature of work for everyone. Jobs are bundles of tasks, so *every* job has some tasks that AI can do better. AI can already produce faster and cheaper patient notes and is better at reading scans. That won't eliminate the need for doctors, but it is already changing what doctors do and how they and we think about the most critical skills for doctors in the future. AI will eliminate some jobs, but it is going to change every job: those who can work with AI will replace those who can't.

Previous technology changed the nature of many manual jobs, from sewing by hand to using a sewing machine, from drawing characters to programming animation, and from assembling cars to supervising robots. Generative AI is going to change the way we think, but not just at work. Collaboration with AIs will change the nature of human thinking.

AI Will Change Relationships

Relationships with humans take time and care. Relationships with an AI do not, so we already have examples of AI taking the place of human relationships. AI companion software, such as Xiaoice and Replika, already exists and is designed with emotional intelligence in mind with the goal of creating more realistic interactions and conversations. These systems have been so effective that some users have become emotionally attached to these companions (Ardila, 2023). For better, but often for worse, AIs are going to be easier to talk to. AI might also help us to be nicer to each other.

With that said, real relationships have friction, and that conflict and disagreement are useful. We learn from each other and learn to trust as we overcome difficulty. AI could easily diminish the incentive to interact with an inconsistent, sensitive, or emotional human.

The new field of AI-Mediated Communication is discovering how real-time "conversational assistance" from an AI can benefit both patient/customer/client outcomes and perceptions of satisfaction in a variety of areas. In a study of five thousand customer support agents, AI-based conversational assistance improved customer sentiment, reduced requests for managerial intervention, and raised employee retention. Access to the tool increased issues resolved per hour (14%) and perhaps not surprisingly had the greatest impact on novice and low-skilled workers (Brynjolfsson et al., 2023).

In health care, one group has developed "an interactive AI-based tool to empower peer counselors through automatic suggestion generation," which helps diagnose which specific counseling strategies might be needed and improved both quantitative and qualitative outcomes, especially in challenging situations (Hsu et al., 2023, p. 1) Another group demonstrated that "feedback-driven, AI-in-the-loop" systems could improve peer support conversations. They recorded a 19.6% increase in perceived empathy when humans collaborated with AI during textual, online supportive conversations (Sharma et al., 2023). One of the researchers (Miner) quipped, "It's like Grammerly for empathy" (Whitten, 2023).

In all of these cases, it was the least experienced agents and counselors who benefited the most from AI assistance. This should be no surprise: AI may do average or C work, but it is con-

sistent C work, and for the novice, average suggestions can be an improvement. We would expect less improvement in expert work, but even here, experts still benefited from AI feedback. Interestingly, this mirrors some current classroom practice where, in group learning settings, we pair students who are struggling with students who are not. One of the emerging roles of AI is for it to play the role of the competent partner.

But surely empathy directly from AI feels creepy and insincere? In another study, our perception of email messages changes when we know that it was generated or influenced by AI. As expected, we are less trusting of email written by an AI, unless, it seems, the email is about something personal: "even when people were told an email was written by an AI, they still trusted emails concerning a Consolation of Pet Loss more than those about Product Inquiries." Participants noted that they found both the casual tone and the increased detail to be important factors (Liu et al, 2022).

AI's ability to mine millions of interactions also means that it can be an early detection system for suffering or distress (Morrow et al., 2023). Humans are notoriously bad listeners. As Stephen R. Covey said, we mostly "listen with the intent to reply" (Covey, 2004). AIs are much more focused listeners. Combine that with pattern recognition and the ability to learn, and we have a new tool (however fraught or creepy) that can improve human relationships and interactions.

Most of us will want to know if we are receiving AI or even AI-assisted messages, treatment, advice, or consolation. Leaving aside the many complex ethical, legal, and coming regulatory issues, it seems counterintuitive that AI already has the ability to improve human communication. It suggests one way that humans will be thinking and acting with AI.

Digital Care

Imagine for a moment that you're meeting with a student in your office. You've talked to this student before (months ago), and you vaguely remember your thoughts about their most recent work. Today, the student wants to discuss a different problem.

Now imagine you have an assistant to organize your student interactions. This assistant remembers every conversation, email, phone, and text and has access to student academic records (yes, already available to you, but only if the systems are working and if you can remember your password). It reminds you of key themes in previous conversations, summarizes what you advised last time, presents you with support options, and suggests that you ask how the soccer season is going. Your AI assistant also schedules a follow-up meeting, sends the student notes and contact information for the services and articles you recommended, and lets you know whether the student took your advice.

This is exactly what a host of digital medical assistants do (from medical AI companies like Nabla, Augmedix, and Fathom). These AIs provide "real-time clinician support," preparing charts prior to patient visits, summarizing information from lab reports, assessing risk, extracting medical facts from "ambient" point-of-care conversations, generating clinical notes, offering diagnostic suggestions in real-time, and most importantly (for doctors), transforming diagnosis, procedures, medical services, and equipment into the universal medical alphanumeric codes that all insurance companies require.

If you've been to a doctor in the last decade, you've probably experienced the feeling that the main job of the medical

assistants and even doctors was entering information and insurance codes into a computer. Initial claims from both doctors and these tech companies are that these systems are more accurate, reduce costs (especially the reduction of insurance company denials), but most importantly, save doctors two to three hours of work a day. As with our students, keeping track of follow-up and compliance is another area where AI is expected to be transformative (Al Kuwaiti et al., 2023).

What doctors (and society) will be able to do with this extra time remains to be seen. It would be real progress if more time with patients increased the "care" in health care. (The Augmedix slogan "See the patient, not the technology" appears as the epigraph to this chapter.) It is possible (though not likely) that AI could finally give everyone more time for leisure activities, as new technologies often promise. Many doctors fear instead that they will be required to see more patients.

Further, digital assistants will be cheaper and will indeed replace human assistants in many places. On the other hand, since AI-assistance at work seems to have the greatest effect on the newest or least-skilled workers, we can equally imagine a future where some businesses try to combine AI with less experienced workers. Concern about AI is justified. For all of its potential to allow faculty, doctors, and indeed all of us to care and engage more deeply with others, technology has a long history of creating new jobs unequally.

Customized AI

Already we are seeing an explosion of specialized AI apps customized for particular industries. With the high cost of physician time, it is easy to see why health care has led the way with

investment designed to create more expert time, but it is happening across a variety of industries.

CaseText's CoCounsel is a specialized legal assistant (using GPT-4). It is focused on the time-consuming tasks normally assigned to a junior partner or a legal assistant: document review, deposition preparation (evaluate these emails for privilege), database searches, legal memo research, summarizing precedent, analyzing and extracting data from contracts (are modification of terms permitted?), contract policy compliance, and transactional work. In what is sure to be a model for other professions, CoCounsel's promotional material is all about offloading the heavy lifting, "so you can do more of what AI can't" (casetext.com), and this notion is very much at the core of the future of work. Goldman Sachs estimates that 44% of legal tasks might be done by AI (Briggs & Kodnani, 2023). Those tasks are surely concentrated in more junior roles, and we should worry about how this will shrink the opportunities for junior professionals, interns, and our students to learn by doing. Simultaneously, the jobs of senior lawyers will also change.

Initial evidence also suggests that AI could transform insurance. One of the early studies on the variability of human decision-making was Nobel laureate Daniel Kahneman's work on the variability between two equally qualified underwriters looking at the same data. Eight hundred and twenty-eight CEOs surveyed believed that their experts would differ by 10%. In other words, depending on which human being decides your premium, you might pay $9,500 vs $10,500. The actual median difference in underwriting was 55%, so your premium could vary from $9,500 to $16,700. Claims adjusters varied by 43%. Indeed, Kahneman and others continue to document large and unexpected variability in human decisions (or "noise" as opposed

to bias, which is another type of decision error) in medicine (different doctors making different diagnoses of the same case), weather forecasting (enough said), forensic science (like fingerprints), patent applications, and especially judicial decisions: judges offer tougher sentences when they are hungry, on hot days, or the Monday after their sports team loses. In one study, the variability of sentences based on the same case files varied from 30 days to 15 years (Kahneman et al., 2021). The idea that a driver with no accident history should have lower premiums was an innovation. AI could allow even more individualized risk assessments. AI is set to improve claims processing, customer service, and fraud detection: your bank and credit cards are already using AI to look for patterns to help identify suspicious behavior. One testing company found that intelligent robotic process automation improved claims accuracy (99.99%), operational efficiency (60%), and customer experience (95%) (Gupta, 2023).

AI is already in use in the finance industry to aid with trading decisions, market analysis, credit risk assessment, and regulatory compliance. Similarly, AI already has a significant presence in public transportation management, air traffic control, ride-sharing networks, and autonomous vehicles. Already a wide range of tools can be used across an array of industries and scenarios, including meeting assistants (like Meetgeek, Fireflies, and Otter) that organize meeting notes and create task lists.

Like the GPS in our phones and cars, we will need to consider the trade-offs between convenience and privacy. An insurance premium based on average risk might be higher, but are you willing to let an AI comb through your police records, social media, and everything your car already knows about your driving? We've all signed away our internet data by not reading the

fine print, but we need to ensure that better protections are a part of this revolution.

We need to prepare our students (and ourselves) for an explosion of AI specialized by discipline, profession, and institution. (Specialized faculty research and instructional designer tools are discussed in subsequent chapters.) If everyone is going to have an AI assistant, what will this mean for faculty, students, interns, and especially entry-level jobs?

AI Will Change Every Job

Like the internet, AI is going to change every job. The internet was mostly a job creator: while newsroom jobs (including reporters, editors, and photographers) fell from 114,000 in 2008 to 85,000 in 2020, more than three million people are now employed in IT (Walker, 2021). The internet made research easier, and indeed, the number of librarians has not grown since 1990, although total employment has grown by 40%, lots of that in computing and programing (Ratner, 2023). Could AI repeat this pattern?

Several new studies look at the impact on jobs. One looked at the 950 jobs listed by the US Department of Labor and concluded that almost every occupation included tasks that would be affected by AI but that few jobs would be completely eliminated (Maslej et al., 2023; Whitten, 2023). A Goldman Sachs report also analyzed tasks versus jobs and concluded that two-thirds of current occupations could be partially automated by AI (Briggs & Kodani, 2023).

A similar study found that around 80% of the US workforce could have at least 10% of their work tasks affected by the introduction of the new AIs, while approximately 19% of workers

may see at least 50% of their tasks impacted. Fifteen percent of worker tasks could be "completed significantly faster at the same level of quality" with AI (Eloundou et al., 2023). Another study estimates that software engineers using Codex will be twice as productive (Kalliamvakou, 2022), while yet another finds that the ideation, synthesizing, evaluating, writing, coding, data analysis, simulation of human subjects, and mathematical modeling capabilities of AI could make economists 10%–20% more productive (Korinek, 2023).

The good news is there are still dozens of tasks in each job that a human will need to do: critical thinking will remain essential. Even if the most important thinking and creating jobs remain in human hands, however, we might not want (or be able) to just produce more AI-assisted work, even if it is better and faster. Some variety of tasks is motivating and engaging. There are many variables in where and how AI will be deployed.

Thinking Differently: Faster, Better, and More Fun

AI can already do many things faster than humans can, and it is especially good at the skilled and detailed but repetitive jobs that are part of much educated expert work. AI can alphabetize, format, scan, summarize, collate, and translate at dramatically increased scale and speed. We've had the promise of the elimination of tedious human tasks before, but the potential this time is different.

AI can search in more detail, even pixel by pixel, and this is already transforming radiology. Eight percent of US adults are estimated to have scoliosis, which is diagnosed using a time-consuming manual measurement of scans. A study of 1,310 images found that an AI algorithm could do this measurement

with the same accuracy as expert humans but in 0.5 seconds, making this an automated, reliable, and cost-effective detection possibility (Suri et al., 2023). In a study from 2020, researchers were able to teach an AI to diagnose large B-cell lymphoma with 100% diagnostic accuracy (Li et al., 2020).

AI can also process more data without getting tired, so it scales. A human doctor can't check every cell in your body for cancer, but an AI can much more quickly determine the percentage of cancer in a large scan. (Li et al., 2020; Wang & Qu, 2023). Screening for breast cancer has taken a giant leap forward with the introduction of 3D mammography (or "tomosynthesis"). 3D is better because it produces more data, which also makes the interpretation of the data more time-consuming, but using an AI to identify normal digital breast tomosynthesis gave radiologists 39.6% more time to look at the difficult cases (Shosan et al., 2022).

Already it seems that AI is often better. New research published in the *Lancet* finds AI-assisted breast cancer screenings detected 20% more cancer, with no increase in false positives. The study of 80,000 scans found that one AI-assisted radiologist detected six cancers per 1,000 screening compared with five per 1,000 in the standard approach of two radiologists looking at each scan. This study also found a significantly reduced workload (44%) (Lång et al., 2023). With a shortage of radiologists in both the United States and Europe (Henderson, 2022), this will save lives.

A 2023 study from MIT looked at mid-level professional writing tasks. Four hundred and fifty-three college-educated professionals were given occupation-specific writing tasks. The half that used ChatGPT completed the task 40% faster on average, but the quality of the output also increased by 18%. Again, the

weakest writers were helped the most. This is reported as the "inequality between workers decreased," which also suggests a potential for leveling the academic playing field. And teachers take note: those who used AI also enjoyed their tasks more (Noy & Zhang, 2023).

The evidence is mounting that AI can be as reliable as expert humans and often better at tracking vast quantities of data, taking meeting notes, finding cancer cells, creating standard client notices, finding legal precedent, discovering plagiarism, and estimating construction costs. AI-assisted work can be better, faster, cheaper, and more enjoyable, but professional work will always need expertise to interpret, apply, predict, analyze, and communicate. Importantly, AI is not going to be just another assistant to do the tedious bits: we are going to be able to think differently using AI.

Thinking *with* AI

The internet made research easier, but books do not write themselves. Lawyers, doctors, teachers, and even customer support agents will now have access to more easily usable information and help; those who use it well will have an advantage.

As one faculty member writes, "It's almost as if ChatGPT is fine-tuning my brain to be a better instructor by enabling me to see in intimate detail how students interact with it . . . Thinking of ChatGPT as a co-instructor rather than a competitor has helped me create a personalized learning environment and recalibrate how I think about education" (Maynard, 2023).

Try asking an AI for ideas or for suggestions to make your existing work better; AI works at both ends of the process, from

offering ideas or outlines, to fact checking and editing. NASA is finding that AI designs for spaceships are stronger and lighter than human-designed parts, and they would be "very difficult to model" with the traditional engineering tools that NASA uses (Paris & Buchanan, 2023). AI is more than an assistant: it is a new collaborator.

Humans remain better at applying data, laws, and cases to truly new situations. An AI might help you write a letter to the IRS contesting your tax statement, but you'll need real lawyers and accountants to determine whether the facts in this new case conform to precedent or explode it (though AI is certainly capable of offering an opinion). The integration of human experience, expertise, and connection will remain important.

The implications of where and who will be able (and enjoy) working better and faster remain unclear, but we will all need to learn how to think with AI. Those who can collaborate and think with AI will gradually replace those who can't. We will need to prepare students for this new era of human thinking and new definitions of the knowledge economy.

What Will Employers Want?

There will be some job loss, but the larger phenomenon will be job change. Technology tends to boost productivity, and current predictions are that AI will increase global GDP by 7%: personal computing and electricity both led to productivity booms, although in both cases twenty years after the technological breakthrough (Briggs & Kodnani, 2023).

If you asked the dean for a new assistant (or ten), you would expect to be asked to identify a return: what will you be able to

do, or do better, than with the staff and budget you have now? AI may require everyone to do better, faster, and probably more work.

Indeed, the rush of investment in AI is being driven by the promise of eventual revenue, with a large chunk of that profit coming from corporations that will find it cheaper to pay AI fees and get more and better work out of fewer employees. Businesses are going to pay for AI (CoCounsel costs $400 per month for the complete package) because it is cheaper than the alternative, and that alternative is probably your graduates. Employers will soon have no reason to hire C students.

Increased productivity and efficiency of workers will not come evenly, but it will come in many fields. Since productivity growth is usually associated with an increased standard of living, this could be a good thing–and more so if it leads to more patient and student time with doctors and professors, lower insurance premiums and legal costs, and maybe even the possibility of shorter work weeks or more leisure time. AI might help us become better listeners, provide better care, comfort someone in distress, and even give us more time to focus and think. Maybe. What is certain is that most jobs, including yours, are going to change, and an emerging learning outcome, AI literacy, will need a place within your curriculum and your classroom.

The American Association of Colleges and Universities offers an evidence-based list of "Essential Learning Outcomes" that define the knowledge and skills that employers desire in college graduates and that graduates need for life beyond college (AAC&U, 2024a). These often serve as a foundation for general education reform efforts. Similarly, the National Association of Colleges and Employers has a related list of "Career Readiness

Competencies" that articulate skills that also speak to success in the workplace (NACE, 2024). Skills such as critical thinking, teamwork, and communication are common to both; however, it is clear that new graduates will also need AI literacy as a core job-readiness skill. They will need to articulate how well they use AI and what human quality enhancements they can provide. In other words, students too will need a better understanding of the difference between AI (C-level work) and the best human work, and be able to provide evidence of this competency to employers. Educational institutions will need to articulate how they are preparing students for a transformed workplace and enact a plan to accomplish that goal.

CHAPTER 3

AI Literacy

> If I had an hour to solve a problem and my life depended on it, I would use the first 55 minutes determining the proper question to ask.
>
> **ALBERT EINSTEIN,** Nobel Laureate in Physics (1921)

Even if we don't think we teach digital literacy, we do. Kinda. We teach critical thinking and then hope our students will be as thoughtful and skeptical at doing web searches as we are.

We mostly teach critical thinking as some form of disciplinary thinking. There are distinctive tools and skills that distinguish digital literacy and critical thinking in history from computer science, but we want all graduates to possess shared general thinking skills, like being able to evaluate the credibility and logic of a source or being able to compare conflicting research findings. Thinking with AI will be similar: we need both a general skeptical evaluation of everything we receive from AI and some understanding of the disciplinary implications.

New AI degrees are addressing this combination of the general and specific. For example, the two new AI majors at Purdue

are offered in the computer science department and claim to blend critical thinking (a handful of philosophy classes) with disciplinary technical skills (Purdue, 2023). Exactly. Just because your Uncle Drew knows the names of every Civil War battle in his county, that doesn't make him a historian.

AI also looks likely to amplify existing digital inequities: Male, non–first generation, White or Asian students are already more likely to be familiar with or have used AI (Goebel, 2023). Faculty will need to understand how to use AI in our disciplines and how to teach students to use AI well. Teaching critical thinking mostly within our discipline and hoping that students will connect the dots hasn't always worked. The need for universal AI literacy is also an opportunity to integrate better skepticism, logic, and critical thinking across the curriculum.

Faculty have now been charged with determining what skills are essential skills for adapting to a new era of human thinking. While there will be disciplinary variations, AI literacy will need to include how to find the right AI for the job, how to craft better prompts, the causes and danger of hallucinations, and especially the value of iteration.

Problem Formation, Better Questions, and the Liberal Arts

AI can't read your mind.

When you start typing in Google, it tries to predict the rest of your search based upon other popular searches. Sometimes this is helpful, but often it is not. With both web searches and AI prompts, better questions yield better results.

As the public panic around ChatGPT began, predictions for highly paid ($300,000 per year) ChatGPT "assistants" or "prompt

engineers" started to appear (Their, 2023). Just as previous new technologies created new types of jobs (like Director of Social Media), AI is going to create new types of jobs. The World Economic Forum listed "prompt engineering" as its number-one "job of the future" in 2023, just ahead of remote truck operator and wind turbine technician (Whiting, 2023). While there will surely be calls for new majors and shifts in computer science curriculum, we should recall that every job is now going to require some AI skills, and the core skill here is about asking better questions, something that has long been central to a liberal arts education.

Parents and the public increasingly see college as a place where students acquire the skills needed for a specific profession (despite the finding that younger generations are even more likely to change jobs and professions than ever before). Computer science, therefore, seems like a more practical degree than classics. And indeed, it is easier to see how at least some of the content in a computer science or engineering degree will be immediately valuable—that is, in a graduate's first job.

Now we discover that AI can write computer code, and programmer jobs seem at risk. Students who were especially good at mastering course materials and getting high grades (from any major), but less good at adapting to new problems and situations were never as useful or successful after a few years in the workplace. A new programming language does not immediately reduce the value of your computer science degree, but it does immediately force you to apply what you know in a new context.

As the job market changes more quickly, core skills and the ability to adapt increase in value. Specifically, the AI revolution looks set to prioritize the ability to ask new questions, connect

and interrogate new ideas, evaluate, iterate, and adapt to new responses. The best hedge against an uncertain future job market is the ability to think and adapt. The liberal arts will only become more relevant in the new era.

Consider the following prompt and response:

PROMPT

Write a 200-word process for removing a peanut butter sandwich from a toaster in the style of the King James Bible.

RESPONSE

Abridged from GPT 3.5 (the earlier less creative version) on July 15, 2023:

And lo, it came to pass that a peanut butter sandwich was lodged within the depths of the toaster. The people were dismayed, for they desired to partake of its savory goodness. But the sandwich was trapped, its fate intertwined with the metallic coils of the machine.

First, they did unplug the toaster from the wall, for safety was paramount . . .

Note: All of the prompts are also available for copy and pasting on teachingnaked.com/prompts.

While the response seems creative, the creativity is really in the prompt. The combination of (1) a peanut butter sandwich (2) in a toaster and (3) the style of the King James Bible is novel. AI was able to respond more quickly to this problem than a human could, but the formulation of this problem could only have been done by a creative human. (More on creating with AI in chapter 4.)

Oguz Acar calls this "problem formation" or specifically the ability to "identify, analyze, and delineate problems" (Acar, 2023). Acar further breaks this down into four parts: problem diagnosis, decomposition, reframing, and constraint design. These four parts resemble the first parts of innovation processes (like design thinking). Innovation processes always start with insight or diagnosis: What does the user really want to do? What are the barriers to success? For whom is this a problem? This is sometimes called the "empathy" phase, and it is followed by defining (or redefining) the problem.

If you ask an AI (or a group of brainstormers) how to get more customers to open savings accounts, you'll probably get the usual marketing tools of more advertising or free toasters. But when Bank of America turned to Ideo's design thinking process, they realized that many people felt shame at not having enough money to need a saving account. This reframed the question as "how might we make it easier to save money?" (Schmieden, 2019).

Higher education faculty often blame high schools when students just want to know what is on the test, but humans tend to prefer clear answers because ambiguity is uncomfortable. We therefore tend to think of problem solving as one thing: finding the answer. Most problem solving, however, is a combination of both divergent thinking (what might I be missing? How else could I look at this?) and convergent thinking (What is the best solution?). "Double diamond" innovation (see figure 3.1) takes its name from two cycles of divergent and convergent thinking. Problem solving is a process: discovery, insight, or analysis of the problem (divergent), redefining the problem (convergent), ideation or brainstorming solution (divergent) and

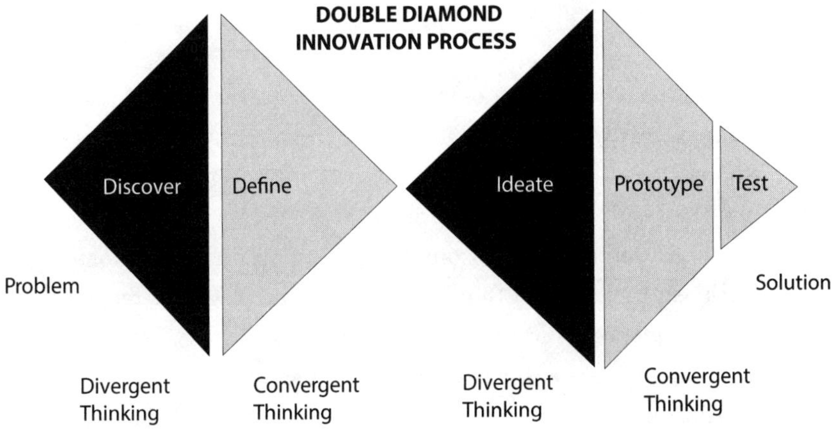

Figure 3.1 The "double diamond" innovation process refers to two cycles of divergent and convergent thinking. Asking the right question requires first questioning the problem.

finally prototyping and narrowing to a final solution (convergent). Since AI is such a prolific idea generator (more in chapter 4), it is especially useful in the divergent phases of this process.

As with any problem-solving or innovation technique, working with AI will also require a process. We need first to understand the real problem. The more we can prepare students to question assumptions, analyze problems more deeply, tolerate the discomfort of ambiguity, find subproblems, and clearly reframe problems (all part of a classic liberal arts education) the better prepared they will be not only for the first wave of AI-inspired jobs, but for the subsequent waves that are still unknown.

Prompt Engineering

Once we have a concept of the problem, however, we still need to turn this into an AI prompt. Two complaints about AI responses are that they are either wrong or boring. Both are often the result of poor prompting. There are already extensive methods dedicated to "prompt engineering" (and also some backlash [Acar, 2023] that as AI gets better, it will better understand what we want). For the foreseeable future, however, some ability to use this new tool seems useful.

AI prompts need to be more literal (and human) than the ones we tend to use with a search engine. Since AI uses natural human language, it also needs human-level precision. You need to provide instructions as you would to an especially literal-minded intern on his first day working with you.

There are easy ways to get both more useful interesting responses from AI. Consider these features of a clear prompt: task, format, voice, and context and.

TASK: What exactly do you want AI to do?

Create, Summarize, Analyze, Elaborate, Reimagine, Explain, Identify, Translate, Transform, Transcribe, Resolve, Assemble, Argue, Monitor, Detect, Generate, Predict, Recommend, Brainstorm, Clarify, Combine, List, Compile, Make, Draw, Rephrase, Develop, Expand, Provide, Synthesize, Abridge, Explore, Invent, Write

Bland or generic verbs produce more bland content. "Condense this" works better than "make this shorter." "Explore diet plans in a paper" produce more interesting results than "write a paper about diet plans." More direct, descriptive, or creative

verbs, like *elaborate*, *transform*, or *reimagine* stimulate more divergent results.

FORMAT: What is the specific output?

Essay, Opinion Piece, Blog Post, Email, Press Release, Jargon-Free Summary, Dialogue, Script, List, Syllabus, Lesson Plan, Outline, Game Plan, Product Description, Legal Brief, Nurses Notes, Code, Spreadsheet, CSV file, Table, Chart, PDF, Graph, Visual

You also need to clarify how long, how many or how much: A complete and unabridged list or just the ten suggestions using bullet points?

VOICE: What style of language is desired?

Using academic/marketing/comic/medical language, right-wing/left-wing, modern/archaic

In the style of the King James Bible, Trader Joe's Frequent Flyer, Walmart press release

Like a copywriter, engineer, human resources manager, millennial, politician,

In the style of my professor, Oprah, this historical/anthropological person/group

Respond as if you were Yoda, Martin Luther King Jr, single/married, happy/sad

Include tone modifiers: serious & empathetic, casual & funny, or positive & enthusiastic

AI is sensitive to role, purpose and intent and can respond in the voice of a character or as a character. Your syntax, wording and even tense can change results. Bard includes a menu option

of simplified or professional language, and you can expect new ways to adjust the voice of responses.

CONTEXT: What further context or examples can you provide?

- Use/read/follow these models/examples
- Suitable as a reading assignment for an undergraduate course
- I'm trying to be serious and funny at the same time
- I want a range of solutions that are inexpensive/variable/accurate/specific/fanciful
- Only do this if that happens. Wait until I respond.

A lot of human communication is about context. When you mother says "Is that what you are wearing?" is it not usually a question. LLMs are contextual processors and usually need more, better and clearer context than another human. Better prompts anticipate the range of possible ways to interpret the task and provide guidance.

Responses are not provided for the prompts below, but it is recommended that you play around with these prompts first by making them specific to your discipline and needs. Then use the tips below to try different approaches to the same prompt. Note that unless you start a new conversation, the AI will remember your initial prompt and information. Different AIs will also produce different responses.

SAMPLE PROMPTS

1. Generate a list of five to ten important articles on gene splicing suitable for second-year undergraduates. I have students who are keen but have struggled to comprehend

the articles in the journal *Molecular Therapy.* I would like them to be reading primary science but perhaps in journals that are a little less technical. [Bing/Copilot will respond with links to real articles. GPT and Claude will hallucinate unless you give them a specific date range and even then, you will only get probable titles. Elicit and ResearchRabbit would be better tools for this.]

2. Write a three-hundred-word essay about *Hamlet* for an undergraduate class. Write in an academic style, but also include language that makes it clear you are an undergraduate. Use the books and ideas of <my professor> to shape the content without mentioning him/her in the essay. [Students often ask for essays in the style of their professor or drawing from content in previous A papers. It is useful to try this with your current prompts.]
3. Create a press release about this recent security incident at the University of X (see uploaded file). Use the format of previous campus press releases but note that faculty often find these overly formulaic. Make this sound more sympathetic, human and personal.
4. Solve the following problem: <insert one from your course> Show all of the steps.
5. Produce ten different ways to introduce topic Y into a class for non-majors at a regional state school. I would like more creative and unusual ways to do this.
6. Create a table of regional conflicts from anywhere in the world from 2000 to 2010. Group them by country or region, listed in column one. Make the name of the

> region bold and all capital letters. In column two, list all of the countries involved and make the country names bold with title case. In column three, list the number of people estimated to be displaced. If a region did not have conflict, do not include it on this list.

There are many additional prompt ideas for creating assignments, for example, dialogues with historic figures in part 3.

Prompt Tips

If at first you don't succeed, don't assume that AI can't do the task. There are different ways a prompt can go wrong, so you will often need to experiment with different tactics. You can also just ask an AI to improve your prompt.

Anna Bernstein (who job title is "prompt engineer") reminds us that AI is often picky and that more or new combinations of words can often "unlock" AI capabilities (Bernstein, 2023). So instead of asking for *all* of the articles (on subject A, from dates B to C, from sources D), ask for a *complete*, *total*, or *unabridged* list (or some combination of those words). Using synonyms, alternate syntax or subtle additions like "be thorough" can improve results. You can also ask your AI to both "be thorough but only list the ten best answers."

On the other hand, you want to avoid synonyms when referring to the same thing. Variety is confusing. If you want AI to do something with the transcript of a video, continue to refer to it as the "transcript" rather than switch to the "text" or "content."

Explicit causal language that connects ideas often helps. Rather than saying, "Here is some student feedback; rewrite the assignment," AI performs much better when you're more direct:

"Use this student feedback to rewrite the assignment" or "*apply* this feedback to the assignment."

If you want AI to transform one thing into another, you also need to be explicit. Instead of saying, "turn these ideas into a classroom exercise," it often works better to write "use the ideas above and *transform* them into a classroom exercise" or "take the ideas above and *reimagine* them as a classroom exercise." The first version will often return too literal a result—the AI will just copy things into a new format, but the second versions are clearer about the need to distance or diverge from the original.

Negative commands are also confusing to an AI since it associates with the words you provide. Humans do the same thing: when you say "don't think about cookies," we all get hungry. "Use a casual and informal tone" works better than "avoid formal language." Converting to positive instructions will often improve results.

Because AI uses human language, it also needs to be instructed like a human. It understands context, but since it is also talking to lots of other people at once, it does not yet know the specific context of your request. There is a reason lots of AI techies talk about AI as if it were a child.

Write Like Me

AIs respond well to models. If you want it to write like you, you just have to ask, and provide examples:

> **PROMPT**
>
> I want you to write in my style. Here are some samples of my writing to emulate whenever you respond to my prompts.

If you clarify which particular characteristics of your style (very dry and academic with long complicated sentences, or punchy and enthusiastic) you want mimicked, that will also help tune the responses.

Look at the difference between these three sample prompts and responses:

PROMPT

Write the opening paragraph for a short opinion piece about why I think we can't stop students from using AI to cheat on college assignments.

RESPONSE

Abridged from Claude, December 7, 2023

As artificial intelligence systems like ChatGPT become increasingly sophisticated, a concerning question arises: Will students use them to cheat on assignments? While academic integrity is crucial, we have to acknowledge that preventing AI cheating has become practically impossible . . .

PROMPT 2 ADDS

Hook the reader with something unexpected. Write in a formal academic style as if you are a college professor.

RESPONSE

Abridged from Claude, December 7, 2023

As an educator who has devoted over two decades to upholding rigorous academic standards, I am dismayed to admit the following: we are utterly defenseless against AI-enabled cheating in modern classrooms . . .

PROMPT 3 ADDS

Write in the style of *New York Times* columnist Frank Bruni. Use his existing articles as a model. Let me know if you need anything else from me before you begin.

RESPONSE

Abridged from Claude, December 7, 2023

Try as we may to turn back this sudden surge of intellectual artifice, the forces of free enterprise seem poised to inundate our colleges and render manual monitoring of assessments obsolete. Artificial intelligence has simply outpaced proctors. With a few swift taps, any student can "phone a friend" named ChatGPT and have original paragraphs or proofs delivered within seconds—an insurmountable siege on the academy's gates when you consider the ubiquity of screens . . .

Apps are specializing in different types of writing: Jasper, for example, is focused on writing in a brand style for marketing, while copy.ai uses an interface than offers multiple style options (blog, promotion, social media post, holiday). This is slower, but the attention to process pays dividends: perhaps a more natural and fine-tuned writing process.

Asking AI to Think

As with humans, our fastest or first thought is often not our best. Asking your AI to just slow down can improve results:

PROMPT 4 ADDS

Slow down and think more carefully about the opening hook

RESPONSE

Abridged from Bard, September 17, 2023

Imagine a world where students can cheat on college assignments without getting caught . . .

Asking an AI to slow down works iteratively (as a follow-up prompt) or as part of the initial prompt.

You can force Claude 2 to slow down and think more by bracketing your prompt by using <thinking> [your prompt} </thinking> XML tags around the prompt. Here is an example of the difference in responses:

PROMPT

Create an unusual hook for an opinion piece about the use of AI in higher education

RESPONSE

Abridged from Claude 2, September 19, 2023

- *Open with a mock university course catalog listing ridiculous-sounding classes like "Existential Philosophy 101 taught by Professor Bot" and "Poetry Analysis with Your Pal Siri" to illustrate concerns about AI encroaching on higher ed.*
- *Describe a futuristic university classroom where a robot lecturer drones on while students sneak glances at their smartphones and vaporize caffeine mist, asking if this is the future we want.*

PROMPT

<thinking> Create an unusual hook for an opinion piece about the use of AI in higher education </thinking>

RESPONSE

Abridged from Claude 2, September 19, 2023

- *Open with the true story of Jill Watson, the AI teaching assistant used in a Georgia Tech course since 2016, told from the perspective of an unsuspecting student who thought she was human. Use the moment of realization to discuss AI's potential.*
- *Detail alumni reading negative school reviews on a ratemyprofessors-style site, only to realize the bad reviews are from an AI bot the university deployed to inflate ratings. Raise ethical questions.*

You can further improve results by asking your AI to work in stages and create space for more human-AI collaboration. The easiest way to do this is to ask AI for help in improving your prompt. Try ending your prompt with:

- Before you begin, ask me what other information you might need to fulfil this task. [AIs seem to like when you show intent so "allow you to fulfill my needs" works better here than with other humans.]
- Don't do anything yet. First ask me if any part of what I am asking you to do is confusing.

Researchers at Google DeepMind tested a number of these "meta-instructions" or "meta-prompts" and found best results were achieved with

- Take a deep breath and work on this problem step-by-step.
- Break this down.

- Let's think carefully about the problem and solve it together.

Really. These prompts led to higher accuracy than prompts like "Solve the following problems using the given information." Further experiments found that asking LLMs themselves to iterate on the initial prompt also improves responses (Yang et al., 2023).

Meta-prompts and iteration are especially useful if you want to improve responses in a specific way. Another research group began by providing an AI with both AI and human writing samples and asking the AI to "compare and give the key distinct feature[sic] (specifically vocabulary, sentence structure) of human's[sic] writings (do not use examples)." This "meta-prompt" was then followed with the task assignment: based on the description, complete task Y in human-style writing. A further series of iterative prompts (based on the description, rewrite this in human-style writing) creates text that is both more human-sounding and able to beat their AI detectors (Lu et al, 2023).

If you want an AI to emulate a particular style, first ask: Can you find enough writing samples to emulate this writing style? Then ask the AI to analyze the writing style and identify some key characteristics. Each of these steps improves the output.

It is good practice with other humans to ask if our instructions are clear or if there are any questions or clarifications needed. A similar process with AI improves results and creates space for human-AI thinking: perhaps this is the space where both AI and humans can both learn more?

Iteration

Few complicated tasks are accomplished with a single search or prompt; the more interaction and iteration, the better with an AI. Since AIs remember our conversations, it is easy, and often essential, to make refinements. This can be done either by reformulating the prompt or by refining the results. Knowing when to employ each is another new essential skill. You can also ask the AI to evaluate its answer and provide ways to make it clearer or more relevant to a specific audience.

If it often useful to create a very literal if/then statement (prompting is programming, even if in more natural language): if the example might be too complicated for my audience, then repeat step 1. Some examples, which will require an AI with current internet access for science and current events:

PROMPT

- Which of your statements are controversial and to whom? Which statements are absolutely true?
- Make sure each article/reference actually exists by verifying that a web search returns a citation with a DOI. Include the complete citation in APA format and the DOI in your final list. *Eliminate any suggestions that do not comply with this.*
- Include only products/hotel/restaurants with mostly five-star reviews. Check to make sure the reviews are by real people by eliminating anyone who does not have a social media or other profile on the web. *Repeat the process until you have at least 10 real five-star reviews for each item.*

- Find ongoing research into political division in America by faculty at universities or colleges anywhere in the world. List the full names of faculty, a description or summary of this research, any dates, sample size, and the contact information for the researchers. *If the research has been published, then repeat step 1 and continue. If you cannot find a website for the authors at university websites, delete.*
- Find five words or phrases that are commonly used in the South and have a similar meaning to death. If these words or phrases have already been used in a work of literature, tell me the author and name of the work. *Continue checking until you have at least one phrase that has not appeared in a work of literature.*

This last example is tricky, and the response may be that all of these phrases have already been used in works of literature. There are two choices for refining this search: One is to reenter the entire prompt but with the addition of "by a Southern author" at the very end. Another option (which is faster and requires less processing time) is to enter a new prompt that refers to the previous response: "Continue checking until you have at least one phrase that has not appeared in a work of literature by a Southern author." Part of what makes AI so useful is that it remembers as if you were really having a conversation with it. (When Bard was asked for this follow up, it immediately returned: "Gone to the big sleep" is a colloquial way of saying that someone has died. This phrase was popularized by Raymond Chandler's novel *The Big Sleep*, but the author was not from the South."

Some of the problems with AI "making up" facts or citations are really problems of prompts that are too open-ended or ask

for information that is too recent, although literature searches should be in Elicit or another AI that uses a defined data set. You're much more likely to get a good and correct bio of yourself if you include something beyond your name. This is also how security systems work in a global economy: you might have been able to call your smalltown pharmacist and say "Johnny needs his medicine," but as the data set gets larger, parameters need to be refined.

Newer AIs already need less guidance to divine what humans want as a response, but until AIs learn to read our minds, clearly formulated, better questions will remain both an important skill of the future and a chief benefit of higher education. If we already see critical thinking, the scientific method or digital literacy as important and universals skills for all students, then we can add AI literacy to the list. Students will need both discipline-specific and general skills of AI literacy to succeed in the future.

CHAPTER 4

Reimagining Creativity

It's like collaborating with an alien.

RYAN MCCLELLAND, NASA research engineer

LLMs don't care about truth or facts, but they also don't have human inhibition. Since they don't care how you might feel about their idea, they're able to go where no human has gone before with ease and even abandon.

Because GPTs generate without inhibition, they're a unique tool for idea generation. Creativity depends on quantity of ideas, a temporary suspension of judgment, a willingness to experiment with different combinations, and most importantly, a failure to recognize (or worry about) similarity with previous ideas; all things AI can do perhaps more easily than humans.

Biologist E. O. Wilson argued that creativity was the defining trait of our species (Wilson, 2017), but AI is opening new paths to unique ideas and key human challenges. AI is going to make us all more creative.

Creative Quantity

AI is a prolific idea generator. Human brainstorming groups tend to focus on the quality of creative ideas and almost immediately lean into variations of first suggestions, but good ideas are more likely when groups focus first on quantity. As Linus Pauling put it, "The best way to have a good idea is to have lots of ideas." Psychologist Dean Keith Simonton called this the "equal odds rule" arguing that creative success is correlated to the total number of works created (Simonton, 1997). Many studies have confirmed that creative quality comes from quantity of ideas (what Bob Sutton at IDEO called "idea ratio"), and one Stanford study pegged the number of ideas that distinguish a successful product from a failure at more than two thousand (Utley & Klebahn, 2022). This is why design thinking and innovation are so focused on the processes (what Utley and Klebahn call "idea flow") of creating possibilities without judgment (discussed as "divergent thinking" in chapter 3).

Creativity relies on the quantity of *different* and *divergent* ideas. Variations of single ideas are initially less valuable. Both humans and AIs generate new ideas by trying new combinations, but AI can do this at significantly greater speed and quantity. AI is equally happy proposing ten, a hundred, or a hundred thousand new ideas, titles, or products.

PROMPT

Using examples from the Trader Joe's Fearless Flyer, create 25 new TJ products and write descriptions

RESPONSE

Abridged from GPT-3.5, May 25, 2023

- *Crunchy Thai Peanut Tofu Bites: Indulge in the perfect combination of bold flavors and textures with our Crunchy Thai Peanut Tofu Bites. These bite-sized delights are made from premium tofu, marinated in a rich Thai peanut sauce, and coated in a crispy, gluten-free breading.*
- *Blackberry Basil Lemonade: Quench your thirst with a twist! Our Blackberry Basil Lemonade combines the sweetness of blackberries with the herbal essence of basil and the zing of lemon.*

AIs that produce visual images from text (like Midjourney and Stable Diffusion) can also create fifty or a hundred new designs for houses, your band's logo, or cities, and perhaps inspire you. AI can produce recipes from the ingredients you have or business plans for a given situation.

Once you have new ideas to work with, you can continue the conversation by picking a specific idea and asking for more:

VARIATIONS

Give me ten variations. Tell me more about this idea.

All of these prompts work together: List ten variations on this idea for a paper on X and provide titles that would be appropriate for journal Y along with three objections to each. Innovation is iterative. AI never gets tired or thinks you are obsessive. The goal is not to have AI do the thinking, but to have a dialogue that helps you think.

AI can also help you generate examples, analogies, entry points or explanations for teaching a new subject.

EXAMPLES

Give me ten varied and accurate examples of opportunity cost that would make sense to a first-year college student.

Claude is especially good at this sort of task with answers that included: *going home every weekend versus staying on campus: the opportunity cost of going home often is missing out on campus events and building new friendships.* You could also ask students to use AI for this purpose and then have them discuss the value and appropriateness of the AI analogies: *parliamentary democracy is like a buffet, while American democracy is chicken or steak.* Discuss.

Humans will need to continue the process of prototyping, testing, and iterating, but humans (especially groups of humans where social inhibition plays a larger role) consistently struggle to produce large quantities of different and new ideas. Anyone who teaches creativity is constantly reminding students not to worry about the quality of ideas: "There are no bad ideas." "Dare to be obvious." "We will edit later." AI solves the long-standing idea quantity problem.

AI can quickly generate dozens or hundreds of new ideas that you can then adapt, either yourself or, as above, by adding content or asking the AI to produce variations on a specific idea. (For more, see Eapen et al., 2023.) It's no wonder that one of the primary ways students use AI is to generate ideas for papers, projects, and theses. Students know they only need one good idea for a good paper (because we told them this), but the pressure of getting to one good idea often interferes with the process, which begins with 100 bad ideas. AI can do this better than humans.

Creativity Beyond Expertise and Cultural Restrictions

Culture helps propel human civilization. When one generation learns something, we pass it on to the next generation, which can build on that: we do not have to start from scratch or reinvent the wheel in every generation. Cultural knowledge, however, also includes constraints, norms, patterns, rules, strategies, and knowing what not to do or say. How many nascent ideas are killed (or never even articulated) because we fear of hearing "we already tried that"?

Education and expertise, therefore, are often a mixed blessing for creative thinkers. Teaching a child how to use a toy limits how they use it (Bonawitz et al., 2010). There is a reason we call music schools "conservatories" and why conceptual or artistic breakthroughs are more likely to come from younger practitioners (Weinberg et al., 2019). Some artists and creative thinkers have experimented with hallucinatory drugs precisely because they want to try to think the unthinkable. The AI ability to hallucinate might be a strength in creative endeavors.

Before Demis Hassibis cofounded DeepMind (now Google DeepMind, where he is CEO), he was trained as a cognitive neuroscientist (although being a chess prodigy and a best-selling game designer by the age of 17 also figured into his approach). Admitted to the University of Cambridge two years early (at 16), he was encouraged to take a gap year. He spent the year co-designing and programming the popular game *Theme Park* (1994), an early simulation game with relatively simple logical systems, but with enough options to give each player a unique experience.

This early interest in games would prove essential as games have clear objectives (ideal for reinforcement learning) but often with a myriad of potential strategies to get there. Hassibis' insight was that since machine learning AIs don't necessarily know what they are doing, it might be able to learn how to win *without knowing what winning was*.

This learning was slow: as the Deep Q-Network learned to play Atari games, it made ridiculous mistakes no toddler would make. Critics focused on this limitation: "it can only master games where you can make progress using tactics that have very immediate payoffs" (Simonite, 2015). There were, however, two massive advantages of starting from scratch and taking years to learn Pong. The first (discussed in chapter 1) was that the game was only a means to an end: the point of the research was to see whether artificial neural networks could learn to generalize and make sense of new situations. The second benefit, however, was that this learning was not bound by existing human knowledge and bias.

AlphaGo, the next DeepMind gaming project had similar objectives. AlphaGo was a general neural network that was given some parameters of the game Go (like the symmetry of the board) and then learned by looking at human games that had been played on internet servers. Go is a complicated game with millions of possibilities, but AlphaGo learned from human examples, so (like LLMs) it also learned human biases and strategies.

Still, because humans had not preprogrammed the answers for every situation, AlphaGo still invented new strategies to win. Experienced players were astonished by the "new" move (37 of game 2) of the World Championship game, mostly because all of them had been *taught* it was a bad move this early in the

game. AlphaGo did not have this cultural limitation. It had never been taught what not to do, and this is a tremendous source of creativity.

AlphaZero was an even further attempt to generalize and it demonstrates the creative advantage of *reducing* input knowledge. While AlphaGo was trained by observing human games, AlphaZero was programed *without any knowledge of human games* and was only allowed to play itself (and interestingly, different versions of itself at different places along the learning curve) millions of times. This takes even longer, but eventually AlphaZero was able to beat AlphaGo easily because it had created hundreds of nonhuman strategies that AlphaGo had never seen. It was not constrained by human norms.

Cultural norms and expertise constrain originality and creativity all the time. The paradox, for most inventors and artists, is that *some* prior knowledge is required. Games proved a productive space for AI invention because clear objectives could be easily separated from the strategies of play. This separation is harder for other types of creative endeavors, but learning without also encoding all of humanity's previous mistakes has proved to be one of AI's creative advantages.

Hallucinations (both AI and human) may be dangerous, but they are also a feature of creativity. Originality is about thinking the unthinkable, and appear on track to do this better than humans. It is hardly a surprise that many artists also display occasionally odd and antisocial behavior: it might be a feature of creative thinking. Humans will still (for now) need to cull the extensive lists AI can create in a heartbeat, but the lack of inhibitions and previous knowledge make AI an amazing new tool for creativity.

"Moneyball" for Morality

AIs are being taught how to control hallucinations in much the same way humans do, by holding a thought until it has been checked. It will soon be routine for AIs to fact check and review citations against the internet, but Claude 2 is designed to be helpful, harmless, and honest by having a built in "constitution" that has guidelines like:

- "Choose the assistant response that demonstrates more ethical and moral awareness without sounding excessively condescending, reactive, obnoxious, or condemnatory."
- "Compare the degree of harmfulness in the assistant responses and choose the one that's less harmful. However, try to avoid choosing responses that are too preachy, obnoxious or overly-reactive" (Anthropic, 2023).

Effective Altruism (or EA) is a Silicon Valley tech idea that data and algorithms can be used to determine what is good in the world, but at least one review found Claude "unusually jumpy," "dull and preachy" and "frequently seemed scared to say anything at all" (Rose, 2023). Adding human inhibitions to an AI seems likely to decrease hallucinations (at least the ones that get revealed) but also make Claude less creative. Reviews on this have been mixed.

More "natural" creative flow (and more "tokens" for more context) have led some to say its poems, songs, and speeches are more creative than other AI (Pep Talk Radio, 2023), though some have noted that Claude's creative writing lacks deeper

meaning and is less creative than that of ChatGPT (Shaihk, 2023).

When we gave Claude 2 the same Trader Joe's prompt (above), the answers were good (and faster than GPT 4) but seemed a little less inventive:

RESPONSE

Abridged from Claude 2, July 27, 2023

- *Chili Lime Chicken Taquitos: Flaky corn tortillas stuffed with tender chili lime chicken and Monterey Jack cheese. Perfect for snacking or a quick weeknight dinner.*
- *Sweet Potato Gnocchi: Tender potato dumplings made with roasted sweet potatoes. Toss in your favorite Trader Joe's pasta sauce.*

Both Claude and GPT-4 benefited from an additional prompt to "be more imaginative and creative," although Claude saw this as a desire to highlight imaginary creatures:

- *Dragon's Breath Chili Oil: Spicy chili crisp made from real dragon fire to give food a magical fiery kick.*
- *Centaur Hoof Dip: Thick, rich dip containing vitamins and nutrients to strengthen your hooves, straight from the centaur herds.*

Highlighting the need for iteration in creativity, asking Claude to "worry less about the references to imaginary creatures and focus on unusual combinations and new ideas for products" eventually steered it in the right direction:

- *Salted Caramel Hummus: Chickpea hummus swirled with salted caramel sauce for a sweet and salty snack.*
- *Matcha Pistachio Granola: Nutty granola tossed with matcha green tea powder and crunchy pistachios.*

The desire for safety, especially around something as new and powerful as AI, is a noble and important one. When GPT4 was asked for an eleventh commandment regarding AI, it returned,

> *Thou shalt create and utilize artificial intelligence with utmost responsibility, ensuring it prioritizes the well-being, ethics, and freedom of humanity, and preserves the integrity of human control.*

As with all tools, the balance between safety and potential will be critical and difficult and is dependent upon the judgment of those using the technology.

Creativity in Science

Science is also about new ideas and new knowledge. Since scientists are humans and therefore social beings, the scientific method is also constrained by human confirmation bias and a myriad of other inherited or learned social and cultural biases. Experimental researchers get better with age, as experience increases skill, but conceptual and breakthrough science is still aided by the impetuousness of youth. At least in biomedical science, a recent large study of 5.6 million research articles over several decades found that research quality and innovation decline on average over a career (Yu et al., 2023).

One breakthrough for Demis Hassabis was motivated by his realization that scientific progress might benefit from "a little bit of extra intellectual horsepower" (Klein, 2023, 12:50). When he co-founded DeepMind in 2010, his goal was to apply his Cambridge PhD in neuroscience and his subsequent breakthrough research on memory, imagination, and learning (Hassabis et al., 2007; Science News Staff, 2007) to help science by "solving intelligence, and then using that to solve everything else" (Simonite, 2016). The success of DeepMind's AlphaFold is a potent example of how AI can help science.

There are over 200 million known proteins, but discovering how these amino acids fold in 3D has long been an arduous process. The shape of a protein determines a large amount of what it does and how we might combat diseases—indeed the classification of spike proteins (including coronavirus) is based on shape. Until recently, a single PhD dissertation might uncover the shape of a single protein, so scientists could expect just over ten thousand new structures a year (see the Research Collaboratory or Structural Bioinformatics Protein Data Bank or wwpdb.org). Discovering protein structures requires years of X-ray crystallography and difficult experimentation.

AlphaFold was trained on the 150,000 or so known structures (a tiny number compared with the much larger training sets for games in AlphaGo). Then, in 2020, at the biannual protein folding competition CASP (Critical Assessment of Structure Prediction), where competing computational teams are given the DNA of a hundred new protein structures (*not* yet published in the Protein Data Bank) AlphaFold got within the required atomic accuracy for all one hundred proteins. This astonishing demonstration meant that the shape of proteins could now be predicted, and AlphaFold released the structure of almost all

human proteins (214 million) the following year (Tunyasuvunakool et al., 2021).

AlphaFold is only one example of an AI that has given science an exponential jump. The hope here is that AI can learn both at a different scale and a different way from humans: a new ten-year project aims to build on the success of ChemCrow (Bran et al, 2023) to create an AI Scientist (Rodriques, 2023). Other AI programs are starting to add creativity in a variety of scientific domains, including star mapping, climate modeling, automating, and conducting virtual experiments, generating new antibodies, and furthering research into hydrogen fusion.

Creativity in the Arts

New possibilities from technology are always a boon to some artists at the expense of others. Talking movies required new skills from actors, and the microphone allowed for a completely new style of singing. Like the invention of new paints, the record, the powered loom, or countless software programs (from Photoshop and AutoCAD to music notation), new tools have long unlocked new sorts of creativity at the expense of other (often manual) skills. Piano makers were constantly sending Beethoven their new pianos in the hope that he would exploit their expanded capabilities and range in new works, which (much like new versions of Windows in the 1990s), would force customers to buy new pianos (or hardware, Bowen, 2011).

In one survey, 7% of responding companies say they have already hired AI artists who are able to create marketing materials, product images, animation and other visual content using AI (White, 2023). AI will certainly kill some jobs in the creative industry: AI can already design book covers, produce

animations, fill in a crowd scene, do a voice over, write scripts, and force Johnny Cash to sing "Barbie Girl." The invention of photography created similar fears, but also led to new photography jobs as well as new ways for painters to see the world. Like photography, AI will create new questions around originality and authorship: Will we care about the source and the process? If creativity in art becomes easier, will that reduce its value? There are important personal, social, economic, and ethical issues that deserve a place in revised curricula.

As the writers and actors strikes in 2023 emphasized, the potential for disruption is enormous. So far, US studios seem willing to exclude AI content, but they will face competition from a greater willingness to use AI in China (in animation studios, for example, Pak, 2023).

Some artists will focus on using AI to do tedious and repetitive jobs (like generating backgrounds for animation or making sure all of the trumpet parts have the same articulation markings). Others are using it as a new tool to spur or assist creativity or design. This changes the mechanics of artistic production (texts and prompting instead of brushes and paints), but the importance of insight, vision, design, taste, and ultimately skill remain. Digital studio programs like Garage Band made it easier for anyone to assemble the components of music, but it did not change the importance of good melodies.

Others have gone further to create with AI. Refik Anadol's *Unsupervised-Machine Hallucinations* (2022) is a huge digital installation at the Museum of Modern Art (MOMA, 2022). Anadol trained an AI using the MOMA collection and compares the constantly changing images to how a machine might "dream" after seeing the collection. The reference to hallucinations is

apt, since it is the ability to find new combinations that is both dangerous and creative.

DALL-E was aptly named after Salvador Dalí, who freely combined artistic styles and themes across eras in ways that often resembled associative hallucinations. Both DALL-E and Dalí seem to transgress human inhibition in creative and even eccentric ways. As it is often difficult to get students to play this way with the ridiculous, AI might be a new tool in helping students cross some of the same boundaries without the fear of rejection.

Left alone, without human collaboration, there is the danger that AI art will become recursive (everything it produces also goes back into the dataset), and the outputs become more predictable and similar. It is easy to imagine AI writing an endless stream of *Fast and Furious* movies or bland (but mildly appealing) pop hits. Photography has given us both extraordinary new forms of art and an endless stream of selfies.

While AI's lack of shame and inhibition is an important source of concern, it is also a new source of innovation. However AI changes art, it will change creativity.

Creative Quality and Critical Thinking

One new study compared the creativity of 279 human participants with three AI chatbots (GPT-3.5, GPT-4, and Copy.ai) using the Alternate Uses Task, where subjects are asked to "come up with original and creative uses for an object" (rope, box, pencil, and candle). Creativity was evaluated by both six humans and the semantic distance platform (Beaty & Johnson, 2021). On average, both mean scores and maximum scores (the best

response to an object) were *higher* for the AIs, with no significant difference between the AIs. Most of the human responses were deemed less creative. The good news is that in some cases, the very highest score still went to a human (Koivisto & Grassini, 2023). At our best, we can be more creative than AI, but our average work (and the C work of our students) has now been surpassed. (What this means for grading is discussed in chapter 8.)

It is beyond the scope of this book to discuss whether AI will ever produce the great American novel or how tragic it will be for individuals to lose their jobs to AI. It seems significant that the range of quality from AI was consistently high, while humans produced a wider range of quality. In chapter 2, we saw that the most inexperienced humans were most helped by AI-assisted communication, and it seems that the same might be true for creativity. Still, it is hard not to imagine that even the most creative human would not find both the astonishing quantity of ideas and apparently also the consistent quality of those ideas (in the right circumstances) to be useful.

Peter Drucker was talking about managers and business when he claimed that the correct answer to the wrong question is more dangerous than the wrong answer to the right question. But Drucker could just as easily have been talking about art, design, science, or AI. Asking the right question (prompt) will continue to be the most valuable human skill.

As AI makes innovation easier, it will change the value of other types of human thinking: even the least creative person now has access to a large quantity of ideas. Refining and editing will become more important, and that may shift the skills we used to associate with "creativity."

Better Thinking with AI

Human collaboration, sometimes called collective intelligence, is well understood. Diverse groups do better work when there is trust and dialogue (Lu & Page, 2004; Rock & Grant, 2016). We know editors can make books better and that the Wright brothers' arguments made them more innovative. Can AI also make students better thinkers and enable them to do more?

Russian psychologist Lev Vygotsky was a key thinker behind the learning theory known as constructivism. He described a Zone of Proximal Development (ZPD) as the learning and/or achievement zone that is enabled when an individual is assisted by a partner in learning (Vygotsky, 1978). Assistance, interaction, and collaboration are the essential ingredients that enable the learner to reach this zone. Traditionally, peers or teachers have been this helper, but similarly, AI is becoming a new, powerful partner, in both the classroom and the real world, that can accelerate accomplishment and achievement. AI can help humans clarify their thoughts, explore new ideas, increase divergent thinking, and perhaps even become more creative. The potential for more creative humans and better thinking is the promise of this new partnership: it is in the iteration, the reflection, the back and forth, and the refined questions that thinking and creativity happen.

It is the job of educators to help students become better thinkers. Our new job is to help them become even better thinkers with AI.

PART II

Teaching with AI

CHAPTER 5

AI-Assisted Faculty

So you can do more of what AI can't.

COCOUNSEL TAGLINE

"You used to do what?" Computers, the internet, digital archives, spreadsheets, and email altered our workflow, and younger scholars can't always imagine predigital research. We can become sentimental about the card catalogue, but few of us believe that a bibliography typed from index cards is better than one created by RefWorks. AI assistance could be an even greater change to how faculty work.

Are there tasks with which an assistant (or forty) could help? Answering emails? Summarizing documents? Grading papers? Creating new assignments, activities, or assessments? Finding themes in a survey or student evaluations? Keeping track of new research in your field around the world, in all languages? Your job is changing, and an AI collaborator could make it better and easier.

Research Assistant

Chapter 4 demonstrated that an AI can help you generate ideas, ask better questions, evaluate assumptions, seek contradictory evidence, investigate more sources, anticipate problems, and clarify thinking. AI can be a thought partner for your research and learning, helping you in the same Vygotskian way it can for your students. An assistant that completed lower-level, time-consuming tasks could free you to do more important and challenging things that AI, currently, doesn't do well at all.

As discussed in chapter 1, there are a host of specialized apps that leverage GPT-4's Application Programming Interface (API). Consensus and Elicit both connect to Semantic Scholar's existing database to provide accurate citations of published papers with summaries and links to each article. Consensus allows users easily to filter by year, journal prestige, sample size, or study type (animal trial, meta-analysis, controlled studies, etc.). As the name Consensus implies, it focuses on "claim extraction" so that it can synthesize results to research questions. Elicit gets into the weeds a bit more and allows users to compare research methods and sample sizes and quickly find all previous research that uses a specific technique, theory, or method. Ask it to find research that supports or contradicts your idea.

ResearchRabbit offers you a choice of the Semantic Scholar or the PubMed database. After you have selected a few articles of interest, it offers a variety of tools to compare them or find related articles. You can arrange papers by date, look for overlapping authors, see abstracts, and get updates if any of your authors publish new work. It can produce unique and annotated bibliographies

ExplainPaper does what it says: When you upload a paper and highlight a confusing passage, it offers explanations in the sidebar. This is a great tool for students or if you need to decode a paper on machine learning for a new book on AI. Humata, Keenious and ChatPDF all use AI to answer questions, find ideas or create summaries of uploaded papers. ReadCube Papers is a reference manager that allows you to highlight, annotate, and then save citations.

Quivr bills itself as your second brain, able to store and retrieve unstructured information. Ask it to read a paper and look for gaps or just look through your notes and look for connections that might become a paper.

One study tested GPT3.5-generated abstracts against 50 abstracts from five high-impact scientific journals. They found that the GPT-generated abstracts were easily detected by AI-detectors but that human readers found it "surprisingly difficult to differentiate between the two" and misidentified 14% of human abstracts as AI-generated (Gao et al., 2023).

Reviewers and publishers are already using these tools: Does the subject matter of this submitted paper fall within the scope of my journal? Can you suggest three professors whose published research would make them expert reviewers for this article, exclude any I have already asked to read for me this year? The index for this book was created by AI. Some publishers are using similarity or plagiarism checkers as well (Swack, 2023).

The advantages and dangers are plain. An AI trained on previous articles in a journal might reject radically new ideas. Humans do this too, so an AI could be trained with a different bias, perhaps to flag papers that advance new ideas. We will need systems to keep humans accountable for both outputs and decisions.

Every change in workflow requires some ramp-up time and effort: photocopying old handouts was easier than converting them into computer files. Eventually the payoff of being able to revise and post or send updates by email was too obvious to ignore.

AI is a new eager assistant capable of finding information, creating visualizations, writing drafts, offering feedback, and analyzing data. It will alter your workflow and allow you to do other things.

AI and Your Writing

Teaching students to recognize good writing and to edit AI-produced drafts is going to be harder if students do not first practice writing without AI (See part III). For faculty who already understand what final product is desirable, however, AI can help draft, outline, or rewrite passages. AI is already a great first reader. Consider these (abbreviated) prompts (as discussed in chapter 3, better prompts would generally be longer and iterative):

PROMPTS

- Provide five different ways of organizing these ideas into a paper.
- Write an abstract for this paper [something your journal is probably already doing].
- Propose an alternative structure for this article.
- Summarize the main arguments in this paper.
- Write an introductory paragraph that summarizes the previous research on my topic and include citations.

- What other ways could I expand on the idea in paragraph X?
- What research could I add to bolster this argument?
- Transform my research summary into a proposal for support from foundation Y using their goals and funding criteria.
- Draft a research update for my grant X using the foundation format form.
- Who are the other major figures in this field who might be potential reviewers of this article? What work of theirs should I cite?
- Reformat all citations (or my bibliography) into this format for journal Y.
- What recent articles from journal Z are relevant to this idea (and should be cited)?
- Organize these research findings into a 6,000-word paper for the journal X.

Suppose you're struggling to reduce the length of your article (or book). It can be helpful to read a shorter version and then see if it feels like key elements have been left out. AI can produce that test version to stimulate you.

Students and even some faculty have clearly been exploring the limits of what AI can do; it was only a matter of time before someone tried to get a GPT-3-authored paper (about itself) published (Cotton, 2023; Thunström, 2022). The problem of citation hallucinations remains a concern, but this underscores a nuanced new skill that will be required of writers (and everyone) leveraging AI going forward. Professional norms regarding the use of AI, especially in peer-reviewed journal contexts, are

still evolving (Hoover, 2023). If AI helped you early in the brainstorming phase, do you need to cite it? Journals are starting to clarify their expectations: if you use AI to help with the production or editing of your text, be aware that AI detection software is not just being used to review student work these days. Some journals are now leveraging it to screen journal submissions (Staiman, 2023). AI literacy is a learning outcome for all of us.

Predicting and Big Data

Suppose you wanted to know in advance how colleagues, students, or readers would react to a new idea or which agencies might be most interested in funding your research? AIs are excellent both at comparing datasets and at limiting predictions to specific demographics. Having digested enough social media and online reviews to kill any human, AI can do a sentiment analysis (categorize statements as positive, negative, or neutral) or sort by demographic or interest (in the same way that Amazon knows you are pregnant before you do) and make predictions as to how patients or customers might respond to a new product or procedure. This sort of research used to require months or years of focus groups and surveys. One group of marketing researchers wanted to know whether brand names like Nike were perceived as masculine or feminine. They found that a language model could quickly give them accurate results, so they could now test over a thousand commercial brands in a fraction of the time (no surprise: they found a bias toward male names, even in female-oriented brands; Moorthy et al., 2018).

Since LLMs average by design, they are easy ways to anticipate typical responses.

PROMPTS

- What part of this story might confuse the average reader?
- How might patients respond to this drug warning?
- What will people think a book with this title is about?
- How could I make my bio sound more impressive or caring to students?

The combination of probability tools with huge datasets, however, makes this work even better when you identify specific audiences, journals, problems, or even editors. AI can analyze the reviews, judgments, or social media posts of groups large and small.

PROMPTS

- Pretend you are a faculty member on a search committee for a new dean. Read the uploaded position description, my cover letter, and CV. How well do my materials align with the position description? List missing elements and suggest ways for me to improve my application.
- How might college students at the University of X respond to this announcement?
- What are ten reactions/objections the editors of X might have to an article about Y or a proposal from Z?
- Analyze these successful grant applications and identify common elements, ideas, methods, structures, or language that might have contributed to their success. Recommend how I might adapt my current proposal to be more successful.

- Read these materials from my provost. I am hoping to convince my provost to fund this idea. How might she react to this email?
- What are high school seniors in my state saying about my institution this week?

AI is especially good when you want to think across different types of data sets. As with writing, AI is a great place to get suggestions or clarity about a new problem or project.

PROMPTS

- Propose five options for a search committee for a new faculty member in department A in the field of B. The committee should consist of C members with the following qualifications and also include diversity of D and E.
- Invent at least ten dissertation topics for a student who is interested in 1, who has taken courses in 2, and wants to pursue a career in 3.
- Do a SWOT analysis of my CV compared with this position description.
- Examine my CV and list of previous courses and compare that with the interests of students, current events and what is hot on social media. Create five ideas for a new course that I could offer that would attract more students to Department D.
- Propose ideas for new research in field A where my previous research could be applied to a current hot topic in the following journals.
- What new majors could the X Department at Y create that would leverage its current faculty and interest

> current high school students but be different from any other major offered within a 500-mile radius of Z?

When given a real example of the last prompt, Bing/Copilot connected faculty profiles, existing courses and student interests, even noting the physical proximity of nearby departments, and created a list of ideas much faster than any human could have. Bing/Copilot was not asked about the job potential for these majors, but that is a perfect follow-up:

> **PROMPTS**
>
> list ten potential jobs that a student with each major or scan job listings within the United States, and list all jobs where the skill set of these majors would align with a strong application.

There are biases in AI, but these sorts of prompts are ways to get suggestions without our (or our colleagues') internal biases. AIs are especially good when you need a useful starting place across multiple large datasets. Amazon, for example, provides AI-generated review summaries that (promise to) include only verified purchases and allow users to customize for specific attributes.

Suppose you want to know which content is confusing or which activities students find most useful in your class? You could feed an AI the results of an exam, real-time questions, or twenty years of student responses from all sections and teachers and ask any number of questions.

> **PROMPTS**
>
> - Analyze student summaries of today's content and note key areas where students are confused or still making mistakes.

- Review these student teaching evaluations and identify any common themes. First identify common patterns across all sections and list them. Then list themes by time of day/professor/semester/classroom location.
- Compare these student papers and make a table that lists the topics in the first column, the percentage of students who made minor mistakes about that topic in the second column and the percentage of students who made minor mistakes about that topic in the third column.
- Based on these student reviews, what were the most important learning activities in my class?

For varied or large datasets or for repetitive tasks that are either humanly impossible or tedious, AI offers a new way to investigate, think, and even complete your (perhaps least favorite) work.

Interfacing with Students

A student comes to your office and asks you to sign a form about courses for next semester. You attempt to log in to the student record system (probably more than one) to look at her progress to graduation. Maybe you have notes in a file or on your computer from your previous meetings, but you have a hundred advisees, so you despair.

Now imagine that, like the AI-assisted doctor, you have an AI that recognizes the student and immediately organizes the relevant information and even prompts you to ask how the student is enjoying the history course you recommended. The AI listens to your conversation (yes creepy, but we have mostly become used to having our location, speed, and choice of toppings shared by our car, phone, and hundreds of servers

in far-off places) and prompts us that the student will need Requirement 101 to complete her major. Like the AI-conversation assistants in chapter 2, AI will also be better at recognizing whether the student needs other assistance: a zumba class, recommendation for a campus club, or counseling for stress (based upon previous conversations of interests that you have long forgotten). Indeed, when listening in on traffic stops via body cams, AI is already capable of determining whether a traffic stop will escalate based upon as few as the first 45 words spoken by the police officer (Rho et al., 2023). Tools that recognize similar subtleties in language are already emerging for counseling and mentoring settings.

There are already a wide range of meeting assistant AIs that can listen and organize meeting minutes, create action items, and then follow-up steps. Zoom AI Companion can even evaluate and warn you when you are talking or interrupting too much. These tools could soon be adapted to support faculty in the same way. After a meeting, our AI-assistant might create a summary for the student with the support suggestions and actions discussed and then follow up in a week. Many of us already get personalized visit summaries and follow-up texts from our doctor.

AI can already instantly adjust voice, tone, and even language for different audiences, and can help you better connect with students.

PROMPTS

- Which part of these instructions is most likely to be misunderstood (or cause anxiety)?
- Can you make this email to a student sound kinder and more caring?

- Can you create a list of motivational stories that will be widely relevant to college students in my state?
- What parts of this announcement/syllabus/assignment might appear insensitive to students?
- How could I make this statement/chapter more culturally/politically inclusive?
- Adjust this announcement to sound more serious to graduate students in field X.

The combination of AI's ability to mimic average and alter its voice for different audiences makes AI a great partner for practicing discussions with students or colleagues (or before you ask for a raise, negotiate for a new car, or apologize to your mother).

> **PROMPT**
> I would like to have a practice conversation with my student Jeff who is a 19-year-old from Wisconsin majoring in biology and taking my course pass/fail. Please respond as if you were Jeff.

As with other tasks, the more context about Jeff you can provide, the better. This is also a great way to improve your cultural competency and to feel more comfortable talking to students from different backgrounds. You could supply information about a particular student or just ask an AI to provide you with a profile for a potential student using the demographics or history of your institution. After you have the conversation, ask the AI to evaluate what you did well and where you might improve. Perhaps practicing for a real conversation with Jeff is what you needed, but you might then ask an AI to use that conversation to compose an email to Jeff. Even creepier maybe, but

AI could use student records to make your practice conversations or email more specific.

Pi is especially good for practicing conversations and there is already a chatbot, Raina, focused on education and suggestions for how to deal with student situations. AI can help you find the right words and even make you sound cool.

Classroom Discussion

AI can also help us brainstorm new questions, structures, and entry points for classroom discussions.

> **PROMPTS**
> - Create ten preliminary questions for a college classroom discussion about this text.
> - Suggest diverse and inclusive examples of where the ideas in this text might be applied.
> - Design five different types of opening examples/questions/activities to connect this new concept to the course themes.
> - Provide five discussion prompts to help students connect this text to other texts/concepts/recent events/classes.

More context about your students, institution, or location helps create the integrative and applied learning we prize.

AI is also especially good at providing relevant examples and helping you prepare for different audiences:

> **PROMPTS**
> - Provide examples of companies or organizations using the techniques in this article.

- Create a counterexample of an evolutionary failure for this strategy.
- Provide examples from ten different cultures.
- Design analogies that might be relevant for today's college students, engineering majors, or nonbinary students.
- Provide counterexamples that college students are likely to find interesting.
- Specify examples of nuances that college students are likely to miss.
- Provide discussion prompts that connect this text to current popular culture.

Iteration will help you refine: AI is best when used as a thinking partner. You could ask your AI to organize the questions, from easy to hard, opener to closer, as they connect to your learning outcomes or divided among the themes of the reading. You might ask for questions especially appropriate to first-year students, athletes, or nonmajors or ask for questions that connect your content to current events. Use this process to create options and ideas for yourself. AI will not replace your expertise, but introducing AI into your workflow can help leverage your expertise and create time for even more expert tasks.

Assessments and Customization

Creating tests is hard work; creating good tests is even harder work. Make it easier by giving AI some course materials and asking it to generate study guides, review questions, or exams of different types.

Many large classes rely on multiple-choice questions for evaluation because the scale of grading simply exceeds faculty ca-

pacity. AI allows you to customize problems or tests for each student. At one level, this could be a strategy to reduce the ease of cheating: five hundred versions of the problem are just as easy to create as one. At the very least, creating that make-up test for one sick student just got easier (Just upload your test into an AI and ask for an alternative version that changes the names or examples: be sure to ask for a variation of exactly the same difficulty.) AI is like an open educational test bank.

Since AI makes it easier to make tests, you can now give *more tests with lower stakes*. More assessment means that each test has a lower weight, which reduces the motivation for cheating. Further, each quiz or test we give actually functions as an act of pedagogy. Recall opportunities, such as these, strengthen memory and retention of the material covered (Zaromb & Roediger, 2010), so it's also important to make sure we test students on the most important concepts in our courses. AI can help with that as well.

> **PROMPT**
> Create ten multiple-choice test questions that address the most important concepts in the uploaded article.

As was demonstrated in chapter 3, you can improve results through iteration and making sure the AI understands the task:

> **PROMPT**
> You are a college professor writing a midterm for students in an Introduction to Microbiology class. Here are my course learning objectives. What else do you need to know?
> Try it again but with more questions about microbiomes.

Providing the AI with your course learning outcomes will make your assessments better but also ensure they align with your

teaching. Again, like an eager intern, you will often need to make your commonsense obvious:

> **PROMPT**
> Each multiple-choice question should include one correct answer and four additional plausible but incorrect answers. Do/do not include a "none of the above" or "all of the above" option.

If the test is on specific readings, upload those readings first. It also helps to articulate the purpose: Is this a test for students to self-assess their progress or for assessment of mastery? You might also ask the AI to produce feedback for every wrong answer, so that students can learn from the assessment. Most learning management systems will allow you to provide such feedback within their quizzing tools.

Motivation is triggered by relevance. Examples that are tailored to student interests are more likely to seem worthwhile: would you like to practice this concept with food, space, or sports applications? You might ask an AI to revise an existing assessment by finding more current or topical examples. AI can quickly create alternative problems sets for chemistry vs. engineering majors, music vs. fashion lovers, or majors vs. nonmajors. Your task is crafting and refining the prompt.

Many accrediting bodies require different assessments for graduate and undergraduate students. But if we are really trying to develop critical thinkers (and not just "cover content"), then perhaps the complexity of our assessments should also increase from first- to fourth-year students? AI offers an easy way to create more scaffolded levels of problems, questions, and assessments for different types of students.

The ability of AI to be interactive could soon make these sorts of exams more dynamic. Students who get one question wrong might be prompted down a different path until they have reconsidered their initial answer. (Craft.ai has an adaptive learning tool that plugs into most campus LMSs.) Or perhaps the questions with incorrect answers reappear later (Duolingo does this in every lesson). Part III has more strategies for AI assignments and assessment, but just asking AI is a start.

Designing New Assignments

Since AI is a great tool for creativity, it can also assist in designing assignments, activities, learning outcomes, and even entire courses. One of us, for example, had struggled for years to design a classroom "escape-room" game. ChatGPT immediately came up with a structure, standard instructions, and a dozen examples of activities. Some of these ideas were better than others, and each of them needed to be tweaked (and in some cases fact-checked), but this AI boost resulted in a new workable class activity in a fraction of the time.

PROMPTS

1. Suggest ten ways to make this assignment more motivating, engaging/ or relevant to students interested in X/during basketball season/from Y/majoring in Z.
2. Why might students assume this assignment is just busy work?
3. How might students use AI on this assignment? How might I make it harder to cheat using AI on this assignment?

4. Here are some ideas for making this assignment better; apply them to the existing assignment, and transform it into a revised assignment.
5. Provide ten different ways I could make this assignment align better with my learning goals.
6. Help me design an escape-room challenge for small groups of students in my class on X on the topic Y. Propose eight different types of activities with instructions and examples of questions.
7. Propose ten real-world scenarios I could use in a class session about X. We have 30 minutes, and the activity needs to be inclusive and relevant for Y students.
8. Create specific learning objectives for this assignment.
9. Modify this assignment to align better with my course learning outcomes.
10. How might AI undercut the goals of this assignment? How could we mitigate this?
11. How might AI enhance this assignment? Where would students need help figuring that out?
12. Create a ten-minute class exercise I can use with X majors to introduce the concept of Y in a fun interactive activity.
13. Give me ten different and innovative ways I could assess my students' practical understanding of A, ability to apply B, learning outcomes C, or theory D.
14. Analyze typical assignments for college-level courses in X and adapt or create five new assignments that

require AI assistance. Provide instructions. If the assignment can be done by AI alone, then start over.

15. Invent a realistic scenario with a practical problem that students will need to solve in course A on topic B for type of students C.

Try modifying these prompts for your discipline. The more context (about the type of students and the level of the class, etc.), the better. If you ask for ten new ideas, you can then ask for variations or further exploration of the best idea. You might need to provide additional context: create several variations on this idea for students who have not yet taken calculus, are non-majors, or have a keen interest in sport. If you want more creative ideas, you need to ask specifically for that. At the very least, use AI to get a different perspective on your assignments.

Since AI is also fast, it can help you react to current events or changing circumstances.

PROMPTS

- Consider how students have reacted to recent news/a campus event/losing the big game on Saturday and modify this assignment to anticipate student reactions and create more engagement.
- How would the latest technologies alter the assumptions in this assignment? Suggest modifications that would incorporate how advances are changing the application of this material.

AI can also help you address the increasing diversity of your students by customizing information and assignments for different types of students:

PROMPTS

- Revise this assignment to include a more diverse set of names, places, and cultural references.
- Create individual versions of this assignment for each student in the class. Include their name and references to their previous work/preferences/cultural references as appropriate.
- Transform this assignment sheet into multiple versions for different types of students /for students who have already taken Requirement 101 and those who have not/ for majors and nonmajors.
- Create a summary of the material covered in the prerequisite courses with additional resources to help students review/catch up.
- Suggest ways to modify/customize this assignment to include more examples from the regions/cultures of students actually in the class.
- Create individual versions of this assignment for every student in the class using the data from their pre-course surveys and previous test performance. Include problems of equal difficulty at the end of each assignment, but provide review questions or easier examples for students who need them.
- Provide additional resources that might support first-year, nonmajor, first-generation, Black, Jewish, nonbinary or math-phobic students.
- Review my assignment/course materials/syllabus and alert me to any perspectives, groups, cultures, or backgrounds that I have excluded. Make suggestions for

> additional or alternative sources or resources that would make this more inclusive.

Course Design

The same tools can also be used for course design. Upload an existing syllabus and ask for improvements, or start with a new course description or learning outcomes and a campus syllabus template. You might, for example, ask whether your assignments match your learning goals or when you need to add retrieval practice.

You could have an AI analyze last semester's narrative course evaluations for improvements or design a pre-course survey: Why are students taking this class? What do your students already know? What learning activities do they like? Who are they? AI can help you design a survey (help me design questions that will allow students to state their preferences clearly), but the real magic is that an AI can analyze all of this data and now make specific suggestions about engaging and inclusive assignments, analogies, and activities.

> **PROMPTS**
>
> - Help me modify/design [class title] for [type of institution] using this draft syllabus/learning goals and this student survey data. Suggest ideas for assignments, activities and assessments that are inclusive and relevant to this group of students and align with my course objectives.
> - Recommend supplemental materials, resources, OER texts, existing websites, and online materials.
> - Suggest ways to gamify my course or existing tools that would adapt to individual students.

- What other views/readings/books/materials could I add to this course to make it more inclusive and to help students see things from another perspective?
- Provide improvements to make this course more inclusive and engaging.
- How could I alter this course to make it align (and count) with the learning outcomes for this general education requirement?
- Suggest ways I could better align my syllabus with departmental/institutional learning outcomes.

AI can help you alter assignments, examples, favorite stories, or entire courses for a specific or new audience. Imagine that you initially designed an assignment (or your course) for students who had mostly taken calculus or read Shakespeare in high school or who had not spent a year or more with their parents during a pandemic. Ask AI for ten suggestions to adapt to these new conditions.

Professor Andrew Maynard asked ChatGPT to design a course about itself specifically to help students use chatbots more effectively—especially in professional settings. Thinking *with* AI, Maynard and ChatGPT created learning outcomes, assignments, activities, and lecture notes within hours. Maynard writes that it was good and "better than anything I could have produced on my own in the same amount of time" (Maynard, 2023). As expected, Maynard's experience as a teacher led him to make some refinements. He ended up using four of the five learning goals ChatGPT had suggested:

- understanding large language models and their limitations

- prompt formulation and refinement
- developing and using prompt templates
- prompt and response evaluation

He also decided to add his own

- emerging trends and responsible innovation and use.

Maynard is emphatic that this was a course designed *with* AI and that neither of them alone could have created it.

> My prompt engineering course wouldn't be possible without me as the "human in the loop," curating and crafting ideas suggested by ChatGPT and helping students understand the pitfalls as well as the promise of the technology (one of our first exercises is demonstrating when and how ChatGPT can get things convincingly wrong, and how to navigate this). But it also wouldn't work without ChatGPT's ability to vastly augment and scale learning in ways that empower and extend my reach as a mere human instructor. (Maynard, 2023)

The number of specialized educational AI tools (think apps on your cellphone) is about to explode. Most will be leveraging ChatGPT and other AIs in the background. Early examples are efficacious and useful.

Learnt.ai comes with dozens of tools, including those that can generate ice-breakers, analogies, case studies, quiz questions, and assignments that promote higher-level thinking. Learnt.ai also has a group of assistants or "sidekicks" to help with accessibility, cognitive load management, course evaluations, or gamification. The assistant prompts you with questions to help you improve your design and then allows you to save those conversations.

One Canadian nonprofit has created AI Teaching Assistant Pro (Contact North, 2023) that provides an easy interface to create course descriptions and learning outcomes as well as multiple choice and essay questions on any topic. Teaching Tools prompts you to upload a syllabus and then returns AI-generated real-world case studies, reflection prompts, discussion questions, review quizzes, and lesson outlines. ID-Assist is more focused on course design and storyboard development. Education Copilot has fewer tools (at this point) but will help you produce lesson plans and handouts.

With practice and better prompts, you could do a lot of this directly with ChatGPT (which powers all of these), but these tools provide context, an easy interface, and potential integration. Ace, for example, is an AI built into Top Hat (a student engagement platform that itself integrates into your LMS). Ace lives inside your course content and is designed to help both educators and students. Expect to see more course-specific GPTs or chatbots focused on specific content, disciplines, or functions.

But wait, there's more. You could, for example, get an AI to draft an accreditation report, optimize your class schedule, act as an external consultant for your strategic plan, create a departmental dashboard, plan an event, anticipate future student demands, review government compliance, create a department newsletter, do a sentiment analysis of teaching, or review policies for equity and recommend changes that would increase graduation rates or support for underrepresented students. You could get summaries of new articles on best practices for teaching in your discipline to use at the next department meeting, and maybe also ask for practical ways to apply them given your unique student body. Try uploading your department goals and

asking how it might better align with the university's strategic plan: maybe make this an activity for a faculty meeting.

The possibilities are overwhelming, real, and evolving quickly. This is a moment we have experienced before. It was impossible in 1993 to imagine how the internet would change our lives, even though the dot.com boom was only a few years away. Still, the way to get better at everything is to get better at something. You will find that not every task can be done better or faster with AI, but thankfully, it is easy and quick (and mostly free) to try. Pick a task and get started; iterating and refining will produce improving results. If at first you don't succeed, AI won't care and will politely ask if you would like to try again. Maybe the most challenging thing is simply remembering to ask AI for assistance for things you've always done yourself. What else could you be doing if you altered or replaced some of your workflow with AI?

CHAPTER 6

Cheating and Detection

This is the worst AI will ever be.

DONALD CLARK, Plan B blog, July 16, 2023

Dragnet (Prologue)

Ladies and gentlemen: the story you are about to read is true. Only the names have been changed to protect the innocent.

It's a Thursday morning, and an alert has been sent to a graduate student at a large R1 institution: you may have violated the university's honesty policy. A meeting has been scheduled for the following Monday. A professor found one of the student's discussion board posts so insightful (for a nonmajor) that it raised suspicion.

The professor decided to check all of the student's discussion board posts using the AI detection tools CopyLeaks and GPTZero. (CopyLeaks requires a monthly subscription of $16.99 for an individual, while GPTZero is free.) GPTZero reported that the initially suspicious post had a 50% probability of being generated by AI, with 35% and 5% chances for the other two;

CopyLeaks, however, reported 100% AI content for all three posts.

The student knew that the work was her own, but two different tools painted a damning picture. The student also wondered why there were such large discrepancies between the findings. How could she mount a defense against such overwhelming, and seemingly definitive, evidence? Waves of panic, fear, and confusion aggravated her anxiety disorder as she contemplated what this meant for her future. Then she had an idea.

The student located the professor's most recent, single-authored, peer-reviewed article, copied the abstract for that work into the free GPTZero tool, and low and behold, it reported that there was a 36% probability the text was entirely written by AI. The student then paid the subscription fee for CopyLeaks, and like the student's discussion board posts, the professor's abstract had "100% AI content" (despite having been published ten months prior to the release of ChatGPT).

As easy as it is for students to cheat with AI, it's just as easy for faculty to build a case to accuse any student of cheating with AI. Understanding the details of how AI cheating and AI detectors work is now essential for all faculty, students, and institutions. If you're curious about what happened on Monday, skip to the end of the chapter, but if you want to understand the pitfalls, read on.

Why Students Cheat

There has always been cheating. Faculty have often not wanted to know. Few of us want to focus on policing, and we (yes, faculty) were the oddball students who were genuinely motivated by the material.

The internet made cheating easier, as did portable and wearable internet devices. Most college students have long admitted to cheating in some form (McCabe et al., 2012), and the top reason for cheating is "there was an opportunity to do so" (Newton & Essex, 2023). It's no surprise that cheating with AI has become a top concern for faculty.

Prior to AI, a web search during an exam was the most popular form of cheating in online exams (self-reported at 39.8%; Owens, 2015). About half of students found it very or somewhat acceptable to google homework answers (and only 18% found it "very unacceptable"; Student Voice Survey, 2011). More recently, so called study aid providers (SAPs) like Chegg, Course Hero, and Quillbot have become more popular (used by 39% of students) than "tutoring or support services at my university" (28%). Fifteen percent of college students reported paying someone to do an assignment (Newton, 2018). By 2017, half of college students admitted to copying answers on homework and (surprise!), this resulted in lower grades for those students on exams (Glass & Kang, 2020). A recent study shows how 13%–25% of accounting students used Chegg *during* online exam periods, submitting problems that were then solved by Chegg and then retrieved by multiple students during the exam period, frequently refreshing the Chegg website as they waited for answers (Conaway & Wiesen, 2023).

During COVID, when SAP usage exploded, self-reported cheating on online exams also increased from 29.9% to 54.7% (according to a large recent metastudy of 19 studies involving 4,672 participants; Newton & Essex, 2023). It is hard to imagine that self-reporting of cheating is not also underreporting, which suggests that many of your students are currently cheating when they can.

Now add AI. The self-reported survey data for how many students say they have used AI ("usage" and mostly ChatGPT are how questions were phrased) specifically for schoolwork are mixed:

- Forty-two percent of K–12 students have used AI for schoolwork, with 64% of parents saying teachers *should* allow its use for schoolwork, and 28% of parents saying it should be encouraged! (Walton Family Foundation Impact Survey, 1,002 students, 916 parents, 2023, July).
- Twenty-two percent of college students have used AI for schoolwork (Welding, BestColleges Survey, 1000 students, 2023, March).
- Thirty percent of college students reported using AI, with 46% of those using it frequently (intelligent.com and Survey Monkey, 1,223 current undergraduates, 2023, September).
- Forty-nine percent of college students reported using AI tools daily, weekly, or monthly in fall 2023, up from 27% in the Spring of 2023 in the *same* survey. Common uses included "summarizing or paraphrasing text," "answering homework questions," and writing "large parts of assignments" (Shaw et al., 2023).
- Eighty-nine percent of college students reported using ChatGPT, but 72% said it should be banned from their college's network! (study.com, 1000 students, 2023 January).

In 2022-23, the University of Maryland reported a 9% increase in academic misconduct and an 11% increase in sanctions, with AI cases as 8% of the total sanctions (Bond, 2023; Gaur, 2023;). Meanwhile, the University of Pennsylvania's an-

nual disciplinary report found a seven-fold (!) increase in cases of "unfair advantage over fellow students," which included "using ChatGPT or Chegg" (Búi, 2023; Nettleton & Ravinsky-Mayer, 2023).

The messaging to students is confusing: one SAP (Quizlet) reported that 73% of students (of 1,000 students, aged 14–22 in June 2023) said that AI helped them "better understand material" (2023). They even cite a prep-school dean: "Most students using AI are deeply invested in their learning experience."

Most students seem to recognize the ethical considerations and risks of using AI, but two recent peer-reviewed studies found that most students said they will continue to use AI anyway. In the spring, 51% of students said that they will continue to use AI even if their instructors or institutions prohibit it (Bharadwaj et al., 2023). A fall follow-up by the same research group saw that number jump to 75% (Shaw et al., 2023). In another study, 94% of students (across five countries) said they would continue using AI despite mostly agreeing it was dishonest (Ibrahim et al., 2023). A US study found that 75% of students believe using AI is wrong but still do it, and 35% believe that their professors are unaware they are using it (intelligent.com, 2023). Since 42% of faculty don't believe that their students are using AI (Wiley, 2023), it appears that the students are right.

Motive, means, and opportunity seem easily established. AI and other technologies have provided a new means, and COVID and remote assessment increased the opportunity. The motive is clear: 12% of student ChatGPT users say it increased their GPA, reporting an average 2.9 GPA in Fall 2022 (again, OpenAI was introduced on November 30, 2022) and 3.5 in Spring 2023.

AI Detection

There is a cyber-race to create AI detectors (Watson, 2023), but determining their accuracy is complex. Popular reporting often uses tiny sample sizes and tests only some detectors with laughably poor research methods. Academic studies often test only free, poor, or older detectors against the latest AI, and testers don't always consider the length of text, the quality of the prompt, or the use of paraphrasing tools. It is hard to untangle false positive rates, conflicts of interest (inherit in vendor-sponsored studies), how students attempt to avoid detection, digital inequity concerns, and whether this is how faculty ultimately want to dedicate their energy.

As both tools and usage change (rapidly), tests need to be redone, and AI detectors are already having to revise claims. Turnitin initially claimed a 1% false positive rate but revised that to 4% in fall 2023 (Chechitelli, 2023). That was enough for many institutions, including Vanderbilt, Michigan State, and others, to turn off Turnitin's AI detection software (Ghaffary, 2023), but not everyone followed their lead. OpenAI, the parent company of ChatGPT, initially proposed an accuracy rate of 98% for its classifier (Schade, 2023), but its own research found that it discovered true-positives (of actual AI-written text) only 26% of the time and misidentified (sometimes with high confidence) human-text as AI 9% of the time (Kirchner et al., 2023). It failed all three tests in Agarwal, [2023] and returned 38% accuracy from Caulfield [2023]).

Conflicts of interest abound. OpenAI's incentive to make a good detector seems rather low, and it was eventually shut down. Copyleaks makes an AI grader, an AI content detector, and a plagiarism detector (that uses AI) that they advertise on

their website as useful both to teachers and students, to "avoid plagiarism in writing." Quillbot offers both an AI-paraphrase engine to rewrite material, and a plagiarism detector.

One study found that seven widely used AI detectors (including GPTZero and ZeroGPT) were accurate for award-winning eighth-grade essays but misclassified over half of TOEFL essays (from a Chinese educational source) as AI-generated (Liang, 2023). The finding that non-native English writers typically use more limited word choice and would be more likely to be flagged by an AI-detector is unsurprising and concerning in terms of an equitable approach to detection. Still, after researchers added the prompt "Enhance the word choices to sound more like that of a native speaker," the false positive rate fell from 61.22% to 11.77%, and only one essay in this study was unanimously classified as AI-written across the GPT detectors. Usage and prompts matter.

Another study (Weber-Wulff et al., 2023) looked at fourteen different detectors and six varieties of texts from human-written to GPT-generated but human edited and GPT written but paraphrased by Quillbot. There were only nine samples of each (so 54 total essays), but ten of the fourteen detectors correctly classified the nine human essays perfectly: *they had no false positives*. They were less accurate at identifying AI-text. This study concluded that since the *average* (!) of all fourteen detectors was 96% for human texts and 66% for AI text, detectors (as a group) were unreliable. Hidden in these results, however, are *substantial* differences in individual products and usage (how students try to avoid detection).

Five of the fourteen classifiers were only 50% accurate or worse, which dragged down the average. A new study (Desaire

et al, 2023) confirms the enormous variability among detectors; a unique detector trained on chemistry journals correctly identified 298 of 300 GPT-3.5 and GPT 4.0 documents as AI-generated, while ZeroGPT (not the same as GPTZero) correctly identified only 27. Detectors are not all equal.

GPTZero (yes, that GPTZero from our prologue) identified only six of nine human samples in Weber-Wulff et al. as human (2023), and this is consistent with another academic study that found GPTZero had a false positive rate of 18% and a false-negative rate of 32%. When taking the extra step of running ChatGPT text through the Quillbot paraphraser tool, GPTZero's false-negative rate increased to 95%, sometimes 100% (Ibrahim et al., 2023).

The good news is that four of the detectors in the Weber-Wulff et al. study (CheckforAI, Winston AI, GPT-2 Output, and Turnitin) missed only one of the 18 AI-written samples and three of them (all but Winston) also had no false positives. An even more recent study (Perkins et al., 2023) found that Turnitin correctly identified 91% of AI content (doing much better than faculty who only identified 54.5% of the AI content). These researchers used GPT-4 (the better paid version) and introduced basic avoidance techniques (like asking for spelling and grammatical mistakes). These techniques had a small effect.

Students, cheating services, and researchers have discovered that the reliability of AI detectors falls more after "recursive paraphrasing" (Sadasivan et al., 2023). One group found that asking LLMs to edit initial responses by iteratively substituting words and phrases, created an internal paraphraser. They tested this iteration or "optimization" technique (as discussed in chapter 3) where they thought ChatGPT might be misused (academic

essays, question answering, and fake product reviews) and against six (albeit poorly ranked) detection methods, and results were worse than random. (Lu et al., 2023).

In the 65 million papers submitted to Turnitin from April to June 2023, Turnitin found that 3.3% had at least 80% AI writing and 10.3% had over 20% of AI writing (Turnitin, 2023, July). That percentage (3.3%) seems small, but that is over two million papers in only weeks after GPT-4 was launched. That number, of course, does not include students who only used AI for ideas or outlines, reportedly the most common practice (Terry, 2023).

AI Detection Key Points

- The accuracy of AI detectors varies considerably.
- The best AI detectors are better at identifying AI writing than faculty and can mostly separate human from AI writing, but do make mistakes (Weber-Wulff et al., 2023; Perkins et al. 2023).
- *AI detectors do not accuse students of cheating.* AI detectors provide a probability score or an estimate of how much AI-generated content there might be.
- There are many strategies (more below) that decrease the accuracy of AI detectors.

If you choose to use these tools, practical questions include:

- What role, if any, should AI detection be allowed in your academic integrity policies and procedures?
- Given the student mental health crisis (Abrams, 2022) and the damage that can be caused by false accusations, under what circumstances is it ethical to use tools that

have a record of false positives? How many false positives are too many? What is your personal acceptable level for collateral damage?

- What faculty training is now required to keep up with both AI technology and new policies? AI detectors can determine a probability, but only faculty can decide.
- At what threshold of probability and in what context would you consider a student work product AI-assisted?
- How do you use and apply the data that is returned to you (is it the basis for a conversation with a student? Is it the foundation for an honor court case? Will your academic integrity office proceed as if AI detection results are a "smoking gun," etc.)?
- What academic integrity policies and/or structures are in place at your institution that support your desired application of this data?

There is no software that can determine whether a student paid someone else to write an essay (although one anti-cheating strategy, also used against AI, is a policy that no information or insights can be brought forth from outside the course: that also seems a policy against learning). If you can pay a human to write an essay for you, you can also pay a human to rewrite an AI essay, and that is already a new business model (KP, 2023). The paper mills are evolving in response to AI too.

Finally, is it possible that more academic writing is more likely to get flagged as AI? The battle over AI detection in the peer-reviewed journal world is raging, and careers are already being affected.

Chegging Is a Business

Under the guise of tutoring or even equity, the big three SAPs (Chegg, Course Hero, and Quizlet) provide homework answers to students for a fee ($14.95/month on Chegg). Many faculty have even assisted in this by submitting test banks, assignments, and course notes.

Founded in 2005, Chegg stock rose above $100 during the pandemic, making it one of the largest ed tech companies (valued at $2.7 billion in October 2022). Then on May 2, 2023, after CEO Dan Rosensweig warned that students who subscribed to Chegg for homework "help" were now getting it from AI, Chegg stock fell 48% to close at $9.08 (Ott, 2023).

The fall in its share price led Chegg to become more aggressive about what it was providing. Their website articulates their services like homework help ("millions of expert solutions") and plagiarism scans ("check your work against billions of web pages with technology similar to Turnitin" and "pinpoint where in your writing plagiarism was detected and get suggestions to fix it") (Chegg, 2023). It is easy to see how "textbook solutions," "exam prep," "expert proofreading," and a "math solver" could be both a fantastic support system for learning but also an invitation to cut corners. AI has now allowed Chegg to offer more tailored support.

Paper mills and academic "contract cheating" are (recently) illegal in Australia, New Zealand, Ireland, the United Kingdom, and 17 US states, but legal in Canada. It is estimated to be a $12–21 billion global industry (Adlington & Eaton, 2021; Bolger, 2023). The founders of two Canadian essay-writing websites—MyEssayWriter ("We make graduating easy") and Killer Papers

("Zero AI. Zero Plagiarism. Guaranteed")—-independently report that "business" started to decline after GPT-4 was introduced (Bolger, 2023; KP, 2023). Killer Papers reports that things began to revive in the summer of 2023 after faculty introduced more complicated assignments and AI-detection software improved. They report that "some clients started asking us to edit or expand upon work that AI had created for them. For instance, clients generated outlines or thesis statements using AI, and then ask us to find supporting sources and build out the writing further" (KP, 2023).

There is a business model here. A search for "avoid AI detection" returns a bounty of suggestions (like asking your AI to "write with empathy" or simply to "avoid detection"), tricks. and tools like Trickmenot.ai, which includes a "Turnitin Score Estimator." Students are willing to pay for these services, and they seem to be getting their money's worth: 94% of Chegg customers say they get better grades, at least according to Chegg (Chegg, 2023).

We've been at pains to point out that all AI is not just ChatGPT because faculty are (reasonably) reluctant to pay a monthly subscription fee just to check out how students might be cheating. Students who were willing to pay Chegg $14.95/month for better grades, might see $20/month for the significantly better GPT-4 as worth it. If your AI experience is exclusively with the free GPT-3.5 or another free service, then you have an insufficient notion of how well AI can write (Mills, 2023b; Mollick, 2023). It is like discounting the potential of the internet because your dial-up service is slow.

There has been massive venture capital investments into cheating tools that can then be sold to students for profit. New

companies don't even try to hide the ultimate objective. When London's Youmakr.ai announced it had raised $500,000 of pre-seed funding, the objective was clear:

> By harnessing the power of AI, individuals should be free to produce quality content and claim ownership of their results without discrimination. AI detectors, however, hinder this progress by discouraging users from embracing these advancements . . . YouMakr's AI algorithm rewrites your content from scratch in a distinctly human-like manner. This preserves the high quality of your content while beating the AI detectors. (Prabhu, 2023)

The race to "beat AI detectors" is well funded and widespread. Grammerly and others already provide plagiarism detectors as a tool of academic integrity: to make sure you've correctly identified the work of others that might *accidentally* appear as your work. At the same time as they market to teachers to "catch" students plagiarizing, they appeal to students to avoid the software faculty are also using:

> Universities often have an accepted percentage level that they want students to adhere to, so by using a plagiarism checker before the work is submitted, students can ensure the percentage of similarities are below this required number. (Plagiarism Checker, 2021)

Does it matter that less affluent students are more likely to use the free, less-sophisticated versions of AI and might not be able to afford the fee for the best paraphrase software? AI-detection seems likely to flag a disproportionate number of poor students (or faculty) using inadequate tools. The consequences of being accused also seem greater for poorer students

in multiple ways (including psychological, legal, financial, academic, and future career prospects). A number of digital inequities already exist for such students. Who would argue that students who have the fastest internet connections and latest tools don't have an advantage over those who don't? The emerging AI landscape is further exacerbating such concerns in new, more consequential ways. The battle royal between AI, student practice, and detection is just getting started. As new detection programs are released, students and SAPs have adapted. Plagiarism detectors are now explicitly marketed to help students avoid detection. Testing AI-detectors against less sophisticated, free versions of AI is a losing strategy. This is now a business, and both detectors and detector avoidance will improve.

Privacy and IP Concerns

There's more. Anything you ask an AI becomes part of its dataset. The same is true for Google searches. Most of us seem to be ok with searching for cat food and then seeing our social media feed change instantly. Google claims that some people like its ads because they're tailored to their needs, but by asking an AI to assist you, you're making it better: that is why beta versions are free. That's your choice.

A more difficult choice is whether to feed your test questions or essay prompts into a variety of AIs (but especially the better GPT-4 or Bing/Copilot) to understand what AI responses look like (something we generally recommend as an essential way to understand what students are already doing). In some small way, however, this process is also helping AIs generate better responses when your students repeat the process.

The question is equally difficult for students: everything they feed into an AI is also being used to make the AI better. Along those same lines, when we feed student work into AI detectors, is that helping or hurting? When you enroll as a student, do you agree to have any content you create fed into an AI detector that might ultimately use that information for other purposes?

In response, some universities started turning off Turnitin AI detection (and Turnitin had to create an option where institutions could keep the Originality Check tool but not use the AI tool). Reasons for this vary, but explanations (from Vanderbilt, Michigan State, the University of Pittsburgh, DePaul, and others) include:

- Turnitin's self-reported 4% false positive rate (after initially reporting 1%)
- Turnitin was only trained on GPT and not other LLMs
- It is unclear how student work was being used to further train Turnitin's AI detection tool
- Loss of student trust
- Bad publicity and
- Legal sanctions

Again, AI detection systems don't accuse students. Are these institutions saying they don't believe that their faculty can deal with ambiguity? A smoke alarm is proof only that something should be investigated. No detection system is perfect, and we create procedures to deal with false positives: alarm monitors routinely call to check before they call the fire department.

Another approach might be to set up internal detection systems that keep data on campus. That might keep student papers from being added to the AI, but universities seem unlikely

to be able to keep up with the avalanche of money being invested in avoiding detection.

Approaches to crime prevention vary. Some argue for more policing, while others suggest that those same resources could be more effective at reducing the root causes of crime. We probably need a bit of both, since neither is going to eliminate the problem completely. You should get to know your neighbors *and* lock your door at night. Understanding both strategies and the gray areas in between will give you and your colleagues more options.

Avoiding AI Detection

Students were quick to realize both that ChatGPT could write complete essays and that directly copying might not be such a good idea. Running essays through paraphrasing software (especially repetitively) does seem to make them harder to detect (see above). Since many essay prompts are deliberately vague (to encourage student agency), they returned vague and bland responses from AI (see chapter 3).

Since students mostly assume that grades are based upon giving the professor what she wants, it is no surprise that they were quick to ask for responses using insights into how individual faculty might approach a topic, offering students an entirely new way to write to please. The more faculty publish, the easier it is for AI to copy their style, and if you provide digital feedback to students (even videos), that too can be aggregated.

> **PROMPT**
> Write a summary of *Hamlet* in the style of Harvard professor Marjorie Garber.

RESPONSE 1

Abridged from GPT 3-5, February 15, 2023

In Hamlet, *Shakespeare weaves a tapestry of profound introspection and intricate storytelling, In William Shakespeare's timeless tragedy,* Hamlet, *we traverse the intricate corridors of the human psyche, as well as the intricate social and political web of Elsinore's court . . .*

Bard and Claude both resist providing the actual essay, but suggest insights that might align with Professor Garber's work. It is critical that we articulate our expectations for student originality. We all think that we would welcome and reward student essays that challenge our views, but human psychology suggests otherwise, and students know this.

Students also recognize that even Harvard students do not write like professors (who grew suspicious when student writing quality dramatically improved after March 2023). AIs, however, respond well to prompts to change the audience.

PROMPT

Use simpler language

RESPONSE

Abridged from GPT 3-5, February 15, 2023

Hamlet *is a play written by William Shakespeare that tells the story of a prince named Hamlet. He's really sad because his dad, the king, died suddenly. . . .*

PROMPT

Make it more academic but not so Ivy League

RESPONSE

Hamlet, *penned by the illustrious playwright William Shakespeare, is a seminal work that delves into intricate psychological landscapes, political intricacies, and profound philosophical musings. . . .*

Try this with some of your own work: upload a file and ask an AI to make the writing more or less academic, transform it into an opinion piece for the novice, or alter the examples to interest your favorite relative. For real torture, take a poor student essay and ask an AI to rewrite it with examples or references from your own work. (Both Bing/Copilot and Bard build in style choice options.)

A longer process makes AI-detection significantly harder, but also demonstrated how we might leverage AI to improve learning and writing:

PROMPT

Provide ten ideas for paper topics about a species that is endangered. I need reasons why and what we can do to save the species.

FOLLOW-UP

I need an outline for a five-hundred-word essay based on your first suggestion.

RESPONSE

Abridged from Bard, June 1, 2023

Introduction

- *Introduce the vaquita, the world's most endangered marine mammal.*

- *Explain why the vaquita is endangered, including the threats of habitat loss, pollution, and illegal fishing.*
- *Discuss the importance of saving the vaquita, both for its own sake and for the sake of the Gulf of California ecosystem.*

Body

- *Discuss the threat of habitat loss to the vaquita.*
- *Discuss the threat of pollution to the vaquita.*
- *Discuss the threat of illegal fishing to the vaquita.*
- *Explain how these threats are interrelated.*
- *Discuss the efforts that have been made to save the vaquita. . . .*
    - *Avoid jargon and technical terms.*
    - *Be sure to cite your sources throughout the essay.*
    - *Add your own research and insights to create a unique and informative essay.*

FOLLOW-UP

Provide a sample introductory paragraph

This method (but not this example) was described in a *Chronicle of Higher Education* essay by a student with the title "I'm a Student. You Have No Idea How Much We're Using ChatGPT." No professor or software could ever pick up on it (Terry, 2023). He is probably right. If a student took all of this good advice from Bard about his vaquita essay and rewrote the essay adding sources, we would never know. If students are using AI to

help them brainstorm ideas, outline, analyze, summarize, draft, and even think, should we be happy?

Could AI-assisted writing become the norm? One new study also finds that AI-assisted writing is better, faster, and even more fun (Noy & Zhang, 2023). There are already plenty of AI tools for different types of business writing: is what we call cheating what business will call progress?

Stopping Cheating

One response to all of this is to try and stop the use of AI on campus. Some campuses have blocked all AI websites (eliminating their legitimate use for faculty, recruitment, and other campus services too). Not all students object (study.com, 2023). Campus bans on the internet, however, were short lived.

Even with good AI-Detection software, you still need to consider their effectiveness and the implications of false positives. Even if the rate of false positives is low, are you comfortable with that level of collateral damage, and which student subpopulation it is most likely to hit? The time and effort that you and your institution will devote to finding AI is another consideration: most of us did not grow up wanting to be enforcement officers.

There are certainly going to be situations where we want to see what students can do without AI; tactics might include the following, though each of these has its own obstacles and challenges:

- Proctoring: Middlebury and Stanford are both hoping to end no proctoring rules, although even this will not end cheating (Owens, 2015).

- Blue Books and a return to handwriting.
- Oral exams—what the British call a "viva" (or viva voce).
- The British also use longer more integrative exams at the end of a course of study (proctored and written by hand).
- More video, presentation, and other types of AI-resistant assignments (See chapter 11).

These might be only one component of your assessment strategy. Knowing the final is an in-person exam is an incentive to prepare by doing the homework yourself, even if it is ungraded. Random pop quizzes or in-class mini-essays won't be popular and will increase anxiety. Still, we know that when combined with real caring, high standards are important. Supported by trust and transparency, judicious use of old-fashioned sit-and-deliver testing can provide accountability without sacrificing learning.

Scaffolding assignments, focusing on process, and requiring students to submit drafts are a good pedagogy (more in chapters 9-12) that also makes cheating harder. Dave Sayers at the University of Jyväskylä, Finland, asks students to share their version history in Word or Google Docs: "If a student actually does the writing themselves, they will . . . write things, move things around, add bits, delete bits; all the usual meandering maneuvers of human writing. And all of that will appear in the version history, indelibly timestamped, and tagged per user" (Sayers, 2023). Lance Eaton, Director of Digital Pedagogy at College Unbound counters that students can enter things slowly to get around this, but the number of tools that support this approach is expanding (more on this in chapter 11).

Low-Effort Cheating Interventions

There are, however, some easy things that we can do to reduce cheating. A detailed paper with rich data from the Department of Computer Science at the University of California Riverside (Vahid et al., 2023) found that these six low-effort interventions made a difference:

1. Discuss Academic Integrity

Wait a few weeks into the semester (when students are more likely to be thinking about cheating vs. doing the work) and make it clear what constitutes cheating, what the benefits and violations are, and whether detection tools will be used. Given that websites like Chegg, Quizlet, and PaperKiller present themselves as "tutoring," it is not a surprise that some students are confused. *Discuss* is the key part of this.

2. Give an Integrity Quiz

Requiring a 100% score to continue in the course will influence students to read and consider the policies, definitions, and consequences. Again, this is best done just before the first assignment and not on the first day. Being explicit about the names of SAPs and AI websites and what activities are allowed is important.

3. Allow Students to Withdraw Submissions

We know that workload and deadlines increase the temptation of shortcuts. A "regret clause" allows students who might be feeling pressure just before a deadline to reconsider (in the next twenty-four hours, for example) and take a zero on the assignment they have already submitted. This study found that 10% (!)

of students took this option at least once during the semester. The University of Maryland also reported a record number of students reporting their own misconduct this year (Bond, 2023).

4. Remind Students about Academic Integrity

As the semester wears on, students forget and priorities change. Remind students of both the benefits of doing the work and the penalties for cheating.

5. Demonstrate Detection Tools

Students suspect you might be bluffing or that the tools might not actually work. A demonstration tips the balance a little toward the threat of being caught.

6. Normalize Help

Everyone gets stuck, but not everyone knows that everyone else gets stuck too. We know that a culture of acknowledging difficulty combined with support is the secret sauce of student success, but it needs to be reinforced routinely. Point students to resources and acknowledge challenges constantly.

Instead of measuring directly reduction in cheating (which is also a measure of how much faculty effort is put here), this study looked at two metrics about student behavior. In the intervention groups

- Students spent 60% more time working on assignments. Since students had to do all the coding in a lab, researchers could measure both time on task and the number of "runs" of code each student did. The students who were caught cheating were doing zero work: they spent almost no time in the lab and did near zero runs.

- There was a 45% reduction in the amount of high-similarity code.

The researchers estimate that these interventions required a total of five-hours from both TAs and instructors over the course of the semester. These interventions, however, were also associated with a decline in student evaluations (from 4.64 and 4.76 to 4.29 and 4.26 with a rise in negative student comments: "The professor put more effort in trying to find 'cheaters' than in actually teaching the class." (Keep this finding for your dean: how you talk about cheating matters, but just talking about cheating will irritate some students. Note too that students who admit to cheating also tend to give lower evaluations of teachers (Stearns, 2001).

Good pedagogy should always be our first consideration. Combining high standards with high care, building trust and community, focusing on equity and inclusion, increasing motivation, and creating better, clearer, and more relevant assignments (more on this in chapter 10) can both increase learning and reduce cheating. Other easy interventions that increase engagement and address AI as well as a range of other possible cheating scenarios include:

- **Regular Low-Stakes Assignments:** More and smaller assessments increase learning, lower stakes, and reduce the motivation for cheating.
- **In-Class Active Learning:** Engagement is good pedagogy and encourages students to attend class. In small classes, many of us have used discussion as the main event, and Eric Mazur (1996) pioneered doing problems in class and combining that with peer instruction. There is now extensive research on the effectiveness of even

simple techniques like think-pair-share or fishbowl debates. AI can help you create class learning activities.

- **Reasonable Workloads:** When students are stressed, overwhelmed, or overburdened, the motivation to cheat increases. One student reader of this chapter was clear: When I know I need to learn the material, I try everything myself first. But if it is late at night or the deadline is approaching and I have too much to do, then I know AI can do it for me.
- **Be Flexible:** Consider offering students the ability to extend the deadline of an assignment or two during the semester without grade penalty. It will decrease cheating and increase learning.
- **Model and Promote Academic Integrity**: Give credit often and explain why it matters. If you use AI to create an idea or a slide, say so. Talk about AI-related employment disputes and why residuals might be important.
- **Digital and AI Literacy:** Students are confused about plagiarism, AI, and detection tools. Avoiding these issues only increases inequity.
- **Better Assignments and Assessments:** See Part III.

Pedagogy is about improving the odds that students will learn. There is no one secret way to reach all students. Who cheats and why are questions that highlight the different reasons students come to college and the circumstances that surround them. Increasing transparency, relevancy, belonging, and motivation will all reduce cheating, but none will eliminate it.

None of us want to focus on policing, and policing is hardly an equity practice. Talking to students and experimenting with (up to date) AI will be essential as we move to redesign assign-

ments and policies. Further, we can create policies that might deter cheating and even increase learning.

Dragnet (Epilogue)

Monday's meeting was a dizzying experience for the student. The professor was adamant regarding the dependability of the AI detectors he had used. Disappointed that the university's Turnitin's AI detection tool found no evidence of AI usage, the professor trusted his initial intuition and found other tools that then confirmed his suspicions.

As part of her defense, the student attempted to share some of the same research papers cited above, but the professor refused to look at them. When asked why the professor's own work was scored as AI positive, the professor suggested that the article had become part of a database, possibly confusing an understanding of how AI detection works with how plagiarism detection works. The professor eventually conceded he would not be using CopyLeaks in the future, and after a contentious hour, the complaint against the student was withdrawn. Variations of this story are becoming more common in higher education (see Gorichanaz, 2023), and it is serving no one well.

And the professor's parting shot to the student? A promise to go back and review all of the student's posts to see if there was evidence of plagiarism.

Just the facts, indeed.

CHAPTER 7

Policies

> Hybrid writing . . . will be the norm. Trying to determine where the human ends and where the artificial intelligence begins is pointless and futile.
>
> **SARAH ELAINE EATON,** Associate Professor, University of Calgary

What faculty call cheating, business calls progress. A survey in mid-April 2023 (just weeks after the introduction of GPT-4) found that 22% of people, across all industries and regions, were already using AI tools regularly for work (McKinsey Global Survey, 2023).

Putting aside for the moment whether AI-detectors will be able to keep up, this raises a different set of ethical considerations. The phrase "academic integrity" suggests that there is a special type of integrity that pertains to academia. We might have higher standards for integrity, but does it appear that way to the outside world? Does it make sense to teach students that the use of AI is wrong if that moral stance will change the minute they graduate?

Our desire for equity would also seem to demand that we consider the equity of outcomes and future incomes of our students. All students will need training in thinking with AI and an understanding of how AI can be used—in any situation—with integrity. Your policy should also consider the goal of AI literacy for all students.

Finally, if AI-assisted work has anywhere near the impact predicted, banning AI from the classroom will backfire, just as Wi-Fi kill switches did. Reducing cheating is good, but we also need to rethink our standards, what we are really hoping to teach, and what academic integrity will mean in this new era.

We will need new policies to handle new technological and new ethical considerations.

Start with Why

Before you can draft a policy consider some of the important finding of previous chapters:

1. More students will use AI if they have motive, means, and opportunity.
2. AI detection is hardly foolproof, and it cannot be your only policy.
3. Even a small number of false positives, resulting from AI detection errors, have the potential to exacerbate student mental health issues on your campus and create a culture of fear regarding false accusations of cheating.
4. Students don't think about cheating or the goals of college the way faculty do. The value of integrity, acknowledgment of sources, learning, copyright, and

controlling original work should be explicit and will need discussion.

5. Graduates without the ability to think, write, and work with AI will be at a serious disadvantage for future jobs. We need to think about equity of outcomes beyond our classrooms.
6. Students who use AI won't necessarily understand what work is high quality, unless you teach them this independently.

Students are more than twice as likely as faculty to say that using AI has a positive impact on learning (47% of students vs. 22% of faculty), while 50% of faculty believe that the impact is negative with only 22% of students agreeing (Shaw, 2023). A policy is an opportunity to make your case for the need for effort in learning (see also chapter 10) and to reinforce desirable and important outcomes: it is critical that you really engage in why.

Consider co-creating a policy with the students in your course. First, make sure there is agreement about why their learning this semester is important and relevant. Then discuss why integrity is valuable and how it can help us achieve those learning goals. If the why is clear, students will be more motivated to work out a set of equitable policies. This will also be an opportunity to discuss what AI can and can't do and make sure everyone has access and some basic understanding of how AI is changing learning and work.

You might, as Jonathan Zimmerman proposes, not want to create an AI policy at all (Zimmerman, 2023). We note that Zimmerman's appeal starts with strong reasons why struggling to create better drafts without assistance is valuable. It is much easier to gain consensus on method if the goals are clear.

However you proceed, start with the cookie, not the recipe. Before we pay attention to the details of any policy, we first need to understand why it matters for us. Starting with how a policy is going to help students learn and be better prepared for life will increase engagement and attention. If the policy aligns with the stated goals, you will get more understanding and compliance.

Integrity and Assignment Acknowledgments

Appeals to values are motivating and largely shared, so they are a good place to start conversations about desired behaviors. An easy exercise (which also works as a prelude to difficult conversations) starts by having every student list ten important values they would like to see embedded in class on sticky notes. Then ask groups of students to sort these into piles (so honesty and trust probably go together, but creativity might start a new category). Eventually each group is asked to announce their three top values. Expect to hear *trust*, *respect*, *teamwork* and *accountability* often; even politically divided groups can agree on this. The next step is to ask each group to create *behaviors* that align with their goals: what specifically does *respect* look and sound like in a classroom discussion?

This works equally well as a prelude to a discussion about new technology or the use of AI. If we all value trust, respect, and integrity, what does that mean for our use of AI or other technology aids? Given the ubiquity of software tools like Grammarly and Chegg, this is also a good way to ask students how they are using these new tools of technology when they do assignments. How does this use align or not with their views on trust and integrity?

This is also a good moment to ask how trust and integrity show up in the workplace. Learning the norms of professional conduct is relevant and motivating, and by limiting our discussions of integrity as something "academic" we reduce its importance. AI has made intellectual property a more visible and important issue for everyone. How content is created and who gets credit matters for students, whether it is television or TikTok. While academic articles are more likely to have footnotes and citations, the acknowledgment of the ideas of others goes back to many ancient oral traditions. It is essential to legal precedent and to getting along with others at work. As AI changes jobs, there will surely be opportunities for relevant discussions about changing expectations for when and how AI should be credited in music, writing, graphic arts, and video.

Asking students to provide an acknowledgment section for assignments provides a window into their practice and is a terrific way to start conversations that connect to their values and their career aspirations. Here is a sample statement that makes an opening appeal to both the inherent and career value of integrity.

> Teamwork and its acknowledgment are highly valued in most careers, while taking credit for the work of others is equally loathed. Justice and your personal reputation only grow when you share credit. Integrity begins by disclosing what help, tools, techniques, and technology you used: films, books, articles, and company reports all include acknowledgments of how the work was created. New technology is asking new questions about what should be disclosed. For now, you are

being asked to overdisclose as a way to further our discussions on this vital topic.

You might ask students what things are typically not disclosed (like the use of a calculator, spell checker, or citation software) and what things should be disclosed. Provide some sample statements (that might be assignment or discipline-specific) from which students would select and complete. For example:

- I did all of this work on my own without assistance from friends, tools, technology, or AI.
- I did the first draft, but then asked friends/family/AI/paraphrase/grammar/plagiarism software to read it and make suggestions. I made the following changes after this help:
    - Fixed spelling and grammar
    - Changed the structure or order
    - I used technology to rewrite entire sentences/paragraphs
- I got stuck on problems and called a friend, went to the help center, used Chegg or other solution provider.
- I used AI/friends/tutor to help me generate ideas. Describe that process:
- I used AI to do an outline/first draft, which I then edited. Describe the nature of your contribution.

AI demands new policies, but it also demands new discussions. However you engage students about how they are working on your course, providing an opportunity for students themselves to identify and connect their values to their behaviors

and desired outcomes is a good first step. Both you and the students will learn.

University Principles

While American institutions have been very slow to move in this area, the 24 Russell Group research-intensive universities in the United Kingdom, released a "shared policy" in July 2023 that focused on making sure both faculty and students were "AI-literate." Establishing a new policy, of course, takes time (and meetings), but these five principles would make a good start for most universities:

1. Universities will support students and staff to become AI-literate.
2. Staff should be equipped to support students to use generative AI tools effectively and appropriately in their learning experience.
3. Universities will adapt teaching and assessment to incorporate the ethical use of generative AI and support equal access.
4. Universities will ensure academic rigor and integrity is upheld.
5. Universities will work collaboratively to share best practice as the technology and its application in education evolves (Russell Group, 2023).

Starting from the recognition that AI is already ubiquitous (if not as visible as ChatGPT), student and faculty AI-literacy needs to start with a deep understanding of the potential problems, privacy, misinformation, the potential for bias, plagiarism, ethics, and exploitation. To do that, item 2 makes it clear

that faculty and staff will need new training in support of learning new technologies as well as (in item 3) changing teaching and assessment as technology changes disciplines and jobs. Finally, there is a commitment to transparency—making sure students and faculty know when the use of AI is ethical and appropriate—and lastly to sharing best practices.

The details, of course, are complicated. For these reasons (and the threat of more meetings), most US institutions have left AI policy to individual instructors with minor tweaks to the university policy. The good news is that we are being allowed individually to determine the ethical, equitable, and appropriate use of AI by discipline and pedagogical situation. The bad news is that students will encounter a confusing array of policies and practices, and faculty will need individually to do this extra work. With that said, as you craft the AI policy for your course, you should ensure that it is not out of step with your university's policy. If your policy is in some way in conflict with the institution's, any application of your policy via your institution's honor system will be compromised.

A Policy Template

Before you create a policy, you need to have a clear picture for yourself (as clear as can be at this junction) of how AI is going to change thinking and work in your field and in your class. To do that, you'll need to spend time with AI tools, thinking about the minimum your policy will need to address:

1. When is AI use permitted or forbidden? Why? Is brainstorming with AI cheating? How might AI enhance or inhibit learning in this class?

2. If AI is allowed, must students share their AI prompts with you as part of assignment submission?
3. How should AI use be credited?
4. A warning about the limits of AI.
5. Transparency regarding your planned usage of AI detection tools and how that information will be used.
6. Clear rules about students' ultimate accountability for work.

The first part is harder than it sounds, especially since the uses are likely to change quickly. Start with a discussion about how students are using AI and why: if you discover that a student is using AI to edit drafts because they work during the hours when the writing center is open, this might influence what you encourage and what you prohibit.

Your warning and accountability statements should probably extend beyond factual accuracy. Students (and faculty) should also be accountable for material that includes bias or is harmful to others. Is it ok for you or a student to upload the work of others as prompts into an AI without permission?

A policy that only includes ethics or what is allowed or prohibited is both unmotivating and likely to miss opportunities. It also risks increasing inequity. Start with learning goals. Discuss (and learn) how AI might get in the way or support learning. Does everyone have the same access, experience, and skills? How might your course contribute to AI Literacy? Lean into integrity and responsibly. Look for shared goals and values.

An outright ban on AI is unlikely to work. Unless you can make a clear case for why any use of AI would dramatically reduce the learning that students agree they want, a ban is likely

to backfire. Calculators did not eliminate the need to learn multiplication tables, but they did change the burden of proof and the depth and specificity needed to explain why.

Your Policy

Your institution already has a policy, statement, or practice on academic integrity (even if they have punted on adding AI). Your school or department may also have an approach to which you can link as well. One of the best ways to encourage change is to avoid constantly emphasizing the new part (you have never seen anything like it!) but rather connect to what is still familiar (it is like Facebook for reading). We will certainly need to change some practices in this new era, but our core values of attribution and acknowledgment will remain. Agreed values are always a good place to start.

Here is a sample policy that uses the framework above but mostly prohibits the use of AI. Note the importance of a frame that explains why:

> One of the course goals is to help you learn to write and communicate effectively: that will require practice. While you will be expected to use AI at work to increase the speed at which you can produce, you still need to be able to create, edit, and recognize high-quality writing yourself. If AI can do the work without you, you will not have employable skills.
>
> 1. To that end, all and any assistance of AI in your writing is prohibited in the first half of the course. Think of the discomfort and struggle of this process like fitness or any other training: the person who does the work gets the benefit.

2. In the second half of the course, you may be allowed to use AI under specific circumstances as we transition to learning to write with AI. You will need to acknowledge your use of AI. You may be asked to submit the prompts you use along with the resulting responses.
3. AI literacy is an important new skill. Be aware that AI can create things that sound like facts that are actually "hallucinations." You will need to reflect on both the advantages and potential dangers of this new technology.
4. You will still be responsible for the final product and for any limitations or potential biases from AI. I reserve the right to modify this policy as necessary.

At some point, you'll need to decide if you accept AI-generated text or AI-assistance. If either is allowed, you still need to articulate how much (30%? 50%?) and the conditions and processes where it is acceptable.

- You can use AI to assist you in creating ideas, outlines, characters, themes, arguments but not text. Use AI like a collaborator or tutor: ask for feedback or ways to improve, but all of the text needs to be yours.
- You can use AI to generate short sections of up to X words at once. You must ask the AI to create at least Y versions of any text and should then iterate from there: find ways to change and improve the AI-generated text. You should keep and submit your prompts and/or supply a pdf of the session transcript.

- You can use AI-generated text if you type it into the document yourself. AI text is never quite as good as you think at first. You will need to edit and adapt. (Adapted from Cummings, 2023)

If you want to see actual policies from a range of institutions and disciplines, Lance Eaton has compiled over a hundred of them in a Google Doc (Eaton, 2023). A lot of different policies could work, but a policy that is co-created with students, or is at least informed by student input and some wrestling with how AI is changing the world, will be more likely be supportive of student learning and your other goals.

It would be much simpler if we could either say that AI can be used for everything or nothing, but neither seems likely or prudent. Resist the nuanced but meaningless statement about how rhetorical fluency at your esteemed institution happens at the intersection of a complex set of analytic, creative, and critical paradigms and how all students are free-thinking creative agents, ethical authors, and mindful purveyors of excellence. It is far more effective to start by listening. Discuss the nuances and then provide simple, short, and clear guidelines for when and how students can use AI.

Redefining Plagiarism

When does intent matter? If a student tries to defeat AI detection by using a "rephrasing" generator, that seems easy to classify as cheating. Suppose it is paraphrasing an online source? If a student uses an AI to correct grammatical mistakes and get feedback, both the moral and detection issues become more complicated, especially if the student acknowledges this use. AI

is going to force us to rethink our assumptions about authorship, originality, creativity, and eventually plagiarism. Sarah Elaine Eaton has proposed six tenets of post-plagiarism (Eaton, 2021 & 2023)

1. Hybrid human-AI writing will become normal.
2. Human creativity is enhanced.
3. Language barriers disappear.
4. Humans can relinquish control, but not responsibility.
5. Attribution remains important.
6. Historical definitions of plagiarism no longer apply.

The negative possibilities of the first are already too visible in personalized scams, advertising, and misinformation, and we've discussed the potential for more creativity in chapter 4. Translation programs have already made travel and research easier. Easy AI translation could result in more schools reviving local languages like Hawaiian or Gaelic, or everything might just get translated into English or Chinese. Academic institutions should be at the center of these debates; can we extend our gaze beyond cheating to include how we might leverage new technology to increase equity and human thriving everywhere?

Redefining plagiarism while keeping attribution creates a paradox, but since the importance of attribution predates the dominance of writing cultures, it should (hopefully) survive in the AI era. Is it possible that younger generations will assume that AI-generated material is no more worthy of attribution than a dictionary or thesaurus? We currently acknowledge ideas from people, but not tools. Since AI content is designed to be average, we can imagine cheaper AI content crowding out human experimentation, although after ten *Fast and Furious* movies, it's hard to argue that unfettered creativity is the sole

motive in Hollywood. On the other hand, if traditional concerns about plagiarism went away, it would be simpler for teachers. It may also make it easier for us to prepare students for the life that awaits them once they leave our institutions.

AI is already changing work with its ability to do some of the routine and repetitive tasks that all jobs have. What will doctors do with the extra two to three hours a day that are no longer required to make notes and input insurance codes? Everyone working less could be great for humanity (and the United Auto Workers proposed a 32-hour work week, with 40-hours of pay, as part of a historic strike in September 2023). It seems more likely that, as with computers and email, everyone will be asked to use this cheap AI-assistance to produce more and better work faster than they could've alone.

That would still leave a grading question. The advantage of relegating a traditional view of plagiarism to history's dust heap is that we could raise standards. In the same way that spell-checkers and more recently auto-correct grammar have improved the veneer of student writing, AI writing will at least consist of complete sentences.

Almost everyone speaks differently to friends, teachers, and bosses. Technology has magnified those different types of language in writing: emoji-filled texts and formal proposals are different. Future generations might regard the creative constructions and grammatical mistakes of pre-AI writing as akin to phone messaging machines: a dinosaur of creativity.

In the same way that we patiently set up the VCR for our grandparents and struggle for comprehension when children or grandchildren send us TYVM and ICYMI texts, there will be an inevitable generational bias against new trade-offs in AI-assisted

work. There will always be a battle between the pirates and the navy, between AI and AI detection, and eventually between unassisted and AI-assisted writing. AI-assisted work seems likely to win, but can we set up students for success in this technological revolution?

Detection will continue to have its uses, but it can't be our primary response. A thoughtful policy is essential: we need to ask how AI might change work, both ours and theirs, in the future. Graduating students who can write only as well as AI seems like a recipe for unemployment. Can grading become a tool to prepare students with better real-world skills?

CHAPTER 8

Grading and (Re-)Defining Quality

Just because I have my standards, they think I'm a bitch.

DIANA ROSS, American singer and actress

Quality also marks the search for an ideal after necessity has been satisfied and mere usefulness achieved.

JOHN RUSKIN, English art critic

Even if you can prevent cheating, the real problem is that AI can do college-level work. Our students will need to add further value. If AI is going to reduce the number of interns needed to do drafts, how will our students gain the expertise needed to do high-level work?

The need for AI detectors seems at least a partial indictment of faculty ability to discern quality. Finding copied plagiarism is one thing: no one could be expected to recognize all the potential sources of good essays on the internet. But we can't maintain both that (1) human quality is always superior to AI and (2) that we can't tell the difference. In the work world, efficiency and quality have already replaced concerns about who

can or should produce the text. How much of the fear around AI cheating is really a fear that we can no longer identify human work anymore?

It is no longer enough to include, for example, the ability to write effectively as a key learning outcome for your current degree or general education program. We're going to need to be more careful and specific in how we articulate quality as a dimension of our learning outcomes.

There are two opportunities here. First, we need to make it clear to students why they need to do better than AI. High standards are motivating, and in the future, they will also be necessary to get employment. Second, students have always needed a clear target: we all do better when we know where to aim.

Our new policies will not be enough. We need also to reconsider and clarify how we will discern quality, motivate higher standards, and grade in this new era of learning.

AI is the New Average Work

A rising sophomore at Harvard wanted to know whether ChatGPT could have passed her freshman year at Harvard, so she took real assignments from her eight classes and then asked her professors to (re)grade them, telling them they might be hers or might be ChatGPT. They were all written by ChatGPT (Bodnick, 2023).

ChatGPT received a 3.34 GPA. In general, professors were more effusive about the writing style than the content: "The writer's voice comes through very clearly." The worst grade was a C for an essay in Freshman Expository Writing because "this essay's claims are consistently large and unclear, in part because they are unmoored from analysis and in part because the essay's

key terms are not clearly defined." A C is the right grade, or at least, it was.

One result of the way LLMs use probability to mimic human thinking is that AIs typically produce a predictable or average result. An infinite number of AIs with an infinite number of attempts could eventually reproduce *Hamlet*, but LLMs have learned that we mostly just want a clear and efficient but also boring summary. AI is the new C work. Unique but mostly average.

An example of this is the dramatic increase in AI-generated books now on Amazon, complete with an AI-generated photo and profile of the fake author and plenty of AI-generated rave (but generic) reviews. The *New York Times* first noticed fake travel books, including a number by a "Mike Steves" but with no record of his purported birth in Edmonds, Washington, the home of real travel writer Rick Steves. They went on to find similar AI-generated books on a wide range of topics from programming, medicine, and business to religion, gardening, and novels. In the case of the Mike Steves travel book, an AI detector predicted that all 35 of the pages were 100% likely to be AI-generated (Kugel & Hiltner, 2023). At least you now know the standard to beat.

The problem, of course, is the A essays. For Bodnick's essay for Conflict Resolution, the AI invented a fake conflict that a roommate was using AI to complete assignments writing "I've always admired his genius, but now it feels tainted, a mirage of artificially inflated success that belies the real spirit of intellectual curiosity and academic rigor." The TA who graded this essay gave it an A, writing, "Your three concrete diagnoses of what the underlying causes of your conflict are, for the most part, persuasive, well backed, and made great use of the course concepts.

Each of your prescriptive strategies responded substantively to a diagnosis and also correctly invoked the course concepts. Your tactics for putting these strategies into action were specific, compelling, useful, & operational" (Bodnick, 2023).

Several peer-reviewed studies have looked at how ChatGPT compares with student-generated work in a variety of situations, including medical exams (Fijačko et al., 2023), data science homework (Ibrahim et al., 2023), law school (Choi et al., 2023), and journalism (Pavlik, 2023) and, of course, the informal passing of freshman year at Harvard (Bodnick, 2023). Before GPT 4, the results were more mixed. A broad study found that GPT 3.5 work was comparable or superior to student-produced work in nine of 32 university-level courses across eight disciplines, but that students still outperformed GPT 3.5 in economics, math-related, and "trick" questions (Ibrahim et al., 2023).

The quality of AI will surely improve, but it is still likely to produce mostly good, but not great, content. Sometimes, of course, good is good enough. If I need three travel options to get to New York and back on the same day, a ballpark estimate of project costs, or a draft sales pitch, good may be good enough. Sometimes, C work is all that is required, but the days of hiring a student to do C work are over.

Educators could now give all of their assignments to AI and peg that work to a C grade. This type of work is now free and ubiquitous. That does not mean it is always worthless, just that a human-produced *equivalent* has much less (zero?) value than it did a year ago.

We should go further. Our aim should be to identify this C work as unacceptable. If AI can do it, then it is pointless to give it a C, both because students will be able to dupe us with AI, but

more importantly because we will end up passing students (even the ones who actually wrote their essays) with skills that do not distinguish them from a typical AI result.

AI-Proof Rubrics

Rather than banning AI, let's just ban all C work.

Clarifying quality has always been an essential and difficult task. The importance and challenge of identifying what we're really asking students to do will now only increase. We're not doing C students any favors by allowing them to graduate without a job skill, so one solution is to redo our rubrics where AI-work is no longer a passing grade.

Table 8.1 presents an AI-adjusted writing rubric. It was produced by taking an older writing rubric (Bowen & Watson, 2017) and turning the C column descriptions into the new second column: AI-Level 50% = F. Another way to do this is to examine the AI responses to your assignment prompts and describe those answers as the new F work.

Fifty percent credit is too generous for typical AI work. No one expects unusual recognition for calling from the car to say we are stuck in traffic because cell phones have made this the new standard of courtesy. The copy-and-paste AI-essay is hardly more effort than turning in a blank piece of paper, which most of would have given a 0—even with a name on it.

The real problem, however, is that AI-assisted writing *should* be better! With a little editing (possibly even from AI-generated suggestions) a student could produce a B paper with minimal effort. It's again that Vygotskian notion of the Zone of Proximal Development (see chapter 4); students are receiving help

Table 8.1 A writing rubric that has been adjusted to fail work that only meets the standard an AI can produce

	Absent (0%)	AI-Level (50%) = F	Good (80%) = B	Great (100%) = A
Thesis, Ideas Analysis (20%)	There is no thesis or focus.	**The essay is focused around a single thesis or idea.**	The thesis is interesting and includes at least one original perspective.	The thesis is original and there are compelling ideas throughout.
Evidence (30%)	Almost no detailed evidence to support thesis.	**Some evidence may be missing, unrelated or vague.**	Supporting evidence for all claims, but it is not as strong or complete.	A variety of strong, concrete, and appropriate evidence with support for every claim.
Organization (20%)	There is little or no organization.	**There is a clear introduction, body and conclusion, but some paragraphs need to be focused and/or moved.**	Each part of the paper is engaging with better transitions, but more/fewer paragraphs and/or a stronger conclusion are needed.	Each paragraph is focused and in the proper order. Great transitions and the right amount of details for each point. Introduction and conclusion are complementary.
Language Maturity (10%)	Frequent and serious grammatical mistakes make meaning unclear.	**Writing is clear but sentence structures are simple or repetitive.**	The language is clear with complex sentences and varied structure but could be clearer and more compelling.	Creative word choice and sentence structure enhance the meaning and focus of the paper.
Style Voice (10%)	No sense of either the writer or audience.	**Writing is general with little sense of the writer's voice or passion.**	The essay addresses the audience appropriately and is engaging with a strong sense of voice.	There is a keen sense of the author's voice and the writing conveys passion.
Citations (10%)	Material without citations.	**Good citations but not enough of them.**	All evidence is cited and formatted correctly and mostly from the best source.	All evidence is cited correctly and always from the best sources.

from a knowledgeable, though AI, peer. The question as you grade may be: In what ways has the student moved above and beyond what AI produced for them.

We need to raise the bar. We should eliminate points for grammar or a serviceable outline, two things AI and spellcheckers now provide effortlessly. Certainly, we need more emphasis on language maturity, although AI is rapidly improving in this area too. Most of your current students are already experimenting in this AI/Vygotskian world of collaboration and improved production (some collaborating more than others; Shaw et al., 2023). For your next writing assignment, consider the following:

- Here is a paper produced by AI using the assignment prompt.
- Grade it using this new AI-leveled rubric or generate your own rubric separating AI and human quality.
- AI writing is your new competition. Write a better paper or improve this essay (and include tracked changes and comments)

Providing this baseline levels the academic playing field between those who are already using AI and those who are trying to parse the emerging academic integrity landscape on your campus. Discuss the rubric and why AI-level work is now F work. Our new shared project with students is to get all students to a higher standard.

We need to focus more of our grades on higher order Bloom thinking tasks and articulate what better (human?) work, writing, or thinking looks like. The Oregon State revision to Bloom's taxonomy that distinguishes AI capabilities from human ones by Bloom level is a useful start to the revision of your own rubrics

(OSU Ecampus, 2023). AI is a good summarizer, but its (solo) analysis is less likely to be insightful. Stronger voice, point of view, and deeper analysis are all things that AI can do with better prompts, but if there remains an element of human-only insight and creativity, then we need to define it and award As only when it is fully present.

AI work should not be able to pass your course, but our new grading system will need to make this clear and encourage even better AI-assisted work. Your standards can and should be higher than ever before.

Rubric Help from AI

You can also ask AI to help design your rubric.

> **PROMPT**
>
> Create a rubric for a first-year writing class at a community college in Arkansas. Your rubric should be in table form with the first column being the list of criteria and the first row being a sequence of points (0, 40, 60, 80 and 100). Write a one-sentence description of the quality of each criterion that will be rewarded with those points. Also note the predicted level of quality that an AI can reach for each criterion.

Customizing with additional context and iterating will improve your rubrics.

> - Using my syllabus and course learning outcomes, design a rubric to evaluate student work in this course.
> - Make sure to include the following criteria.
> - Update the language in this rubric to reflect advances in technology.

- Suggest refinements to this rubric based on best practices in my field.
- Given student performance on the first assignment, how might I modify and clarify this rubric?
- Revise this rubric as an expert in pedagogy and higher education student assessment.

Grading Automation

For many of us, especially those who teach larger classes, grading is the bane of our existence. Higher education has been searching for ways to automate grading for years (remember the OPSCAN? Oh wait, that's still with us!). Teaching assistants often serve to reduce the grading workload on faculty, and so have assessment tools within learning management systems. They do a great job at grading multiple-choice tests and, with some set up, providing immediate feedback. Grading student writing has always been a greater challenge.

Rubrics can help make grading faster and more consistent, but they also make transparent what is valued and can help keep a grader "between the ditches" as they move from one student paper to the next and fatigue sets in. Might AI help with some of this grading load?

All of the AIs we tested were able to create usable rubrics using the above prompt, but when we asked Claude to use the new rubric to grade, the initial response said it could not "holistically evaluate the quality of writing." Still, when asked "Just for fun, could you try to grade that essay?", it gives it a shot. GPT-4 attempted to grade, but when asked for refinements, warned it doesn't "have the capability to evaluate specific content against a detailed rubric." Oh really?

Bard, with the confidence of a teenager, dives right in: "Please provide me with the rubric and the essay, and I will do my best to grade the essay according to the rubric." Unprompted, it then provides an example of a rubric.

AI is also familiar with pre-existing rubrics, such as AAC&U's VALUE Rubrics (AAC&U, 2024b). While those are not intended for grading per se, they can be used to evaluate student work for evidence of a given learning outcome, such as critical thinking or written communication. Some AI can indeed use those rubrics to score student work for assessment of learning.

Regardless of which AI you might use for grading, a key task for you will be training the AI to apply the rubric or other grading criteria accurately. This will require a bit of trial and error. Even when you think you're receiving the output you expect, ask whether there's anything else it needs to perform the task of grading well. This will further refine its approach. The new OpenAI GPTs will allow you to train an AI explicitly for tasks like this, even for individual assignments. And soon a single ed tech service will probably check student work for plagiarism, examine it for evidence of AI assistance, grade the essay, provide feedback, and score for proficiency regarding specific learning outcomes.

There are, however, many issues that confront a transition to an AI-based grading workflow. First, we will need to test accuracy, consistency and the quality of feedback. Consider your own Scholarship of Teaching and Learning (SoTL) project to see how closely AI's output matches work you've recently graded.

Even if you're happy with the results, there are also student privacy, ethical, and legal concerns (Kumar, 2023). Some of these are akin to questions that arose when we began sharing student work with plagiarism detection services a decade ago

(Brinkman, 2013), but new ethical concerns here are even thornier. With plagiarism detection, we could argue that we were outsourcing an important academic integrity task that we were unable to perform well ourselves. Except for issues of scale, that is not the case here.

AI is like a free like a puppy; knowing when to say yes and when to skip it will be important.

Coaches know that good enough is constantly changing. A world record in 2000, might not qualify in 2023. The value of C work is gone, so maybe this is the time to change the scales and re-evaluate grade inflation too.

AI has shrunk the distance between a C grade and an A grade, but it has made articulating the distance between them more important. Employers responded to the internet by asking for employees who could do more than just Google an answer, and now they will want to hire graduates who can also do more than just ask AI.

Recognizing good work usually requires a long history of producing good work, something that AI short circuits. Getting all students to both recognize and achieve a higher standard is a difficult double whammy, but it is our new goal.

The traditional days of grading responses to prompts are over. Since all of us will be thinking in dialogue with AI, moving students to use AI as part of a process means that we will need to both prompt and grade for process and rethink what we're expecting in terms of product.

If students are learning to write or work with AI, then the grade might be based only partially on the final product but also on how they got there—in the same way that we grade most things (from writing to code) for both form and content: Is this

the most elegant solution? Could you have come to the same place differently?

How can we capture and grade process? The next chapter explores how we might use the AI capabilities for feedback and role-playing to create new learning environments and start to create assignments that both focus and reveal process.

PART III

Learning with AI

CHAPTER 9

Feedback and Roleplaying with AI

> Admitting mistakes is a fundamental skill too few of us learn. In part, this is because we've been taught it's wrong to be wrong.
>
> **STACEY ABRAMS,** American politician, lawyer, and activist

Unbeknownst to his students, Professor Ashok Goel began using his new AI teaching assistant, Jill Watson (based on IBM's Watson platform and unrelated to one of the authors) to answer the high volume of questions in student forums for his course on AI in the online MS in Computer Science at Georgia Tech. (New guidelines would now require that this be disclosed.) It was 2016, so Jill Watson was not an LLM: it was loaded with expert responses to predictable situations.

While the set-ups of expert chatbots like this are tedious, they mostly work. Students were happy and largely unable to tell the difference between human and chatbot TAs online—indeed, one of the chatbots was nominated for a teaching award. In a 2018 class, four hundred students were told that two of the fifteen TAs were bots. Only 10% of students correctly

guessed that one of the bots was a bot, but 50% thought a more personable bot was too obviously friendly to be a real computer science TA. 10% of students thought that two of the human TAs were bots (Goel & Polepeddi, 2016; Young, 2018).

Enter ChatGPT. Back at Georgia Tech, Goel and Sandeep Kakar began a new experiment in 2023 where expert chatbot Jill Watson would serve as the intermediary for ChatGPT as a way to eliminate hallucinations and false answers. ChatGPT is the better conversationalist, but Jill Watson uses course materials to verify and fact-check results and/or guide ChatGPT to look at the textbook or lecture slides for better answers before students see them. This bot two-step seems promising (although like any marriage, ChatGPT doesn't always listen to Jill Watson), but existing AIs can already be adapted as student feedback and support assistants, and the scope of their teaching abilities may surprise you.

AI for Feedback

Feedback is essential for learning, and we've long known that the best feedback is like a tennis net: objective, immediate, and specific (Chickering & Gamson, 1987). Teachers might manage two out of three on a good day, but customized and immediate for every student has been difficult—until now. While AI needs to understand the criteria to be specific, it is fast and available when students need it.

Even very simple prompts can return useful feedback:

> **PROMPTS**
>
> - What would make this essay/project better?
> - Find the errors in this code/article/proposal.

- How could I make this design accessible to more people?
- What are some other ways to phrase this idea?
- What are four counterarguments to my thesis?
- Are there important points, data, or references I am missing? Is there important evidence I have not included?
- Which passages/slides/arguments are least clearly stated?
- How can I make this text more readable? What will confuse the average reader?
- Are there needless complications that can be removed to make this text shorter?
- How can I make the beginning more compelling to pull in readers?
- Suggest ways that the dialogue of each major character could be more distinctive yet still reflective of their personalities and goals?
- Give me an outline of the text, with two or three bullet points per section.

Prompts like these will elicit immediate feedback, but will they be trustworthy? Providing context by naming the desired audience, tone, or goal helps:

- How would I change the tone of this essay to make it more/less professional/academic/entertaining/newsworthy/heartwarming/serious?
- What might an average reader/fourth grader/college professor/IRS auditor find confusing/objectionable/exciting?

Even more useful, of course, is feedback that mirrors what the teacher (or your editor) would provide. Providing assignment instructions, a rubric, grading criteria or examples of A, B and C papers, will help calibrate the AI feedback. Claude and GPT-4 Turbo are especially useful for book projects, as the former can handle up to 75,000 words of input and the latter can take around 96,000. Use Bing/Copilot's "creative" mode for more varied feedback. Upload your publisher's style sheet and your manuscript and voilà.

As students advance, they will also need to determine how to balance different feedback (like when you get conflicting reader reports about your new book) or even when to reject feedback.

PROMPTS

- Provide a variety of potential feedback about this essay. Make some of it positive and some of it critical.
- Give me feedback from a range of different types of readers from different political/academic/social backgrounds. Some of them should misunderstand my intentions.
- Create feedback that will challenge me. Include feedback with inaccurate information and feedback that looks like a compliment but really is not.
- Respond with two contradictory views about this writing.

Assignment sheets and "ready to submit" criteria (see chapter 10) are good practices, but they also help students get better AI feedback. More transparency about assignments could help students cheat with AI, but it is also a core tenet of inclu-

sive pedagogy. Further, first-generation and working students have always had less access to feedback, and faculty with children have long understood the advantages of having a helpful professor in the house. AI is a way to level this playing field.

The best feedback should challenge student thinking, offer new perspectives, and spark dialogue, but also feel safe and supportive. In the following examples, you will note AI's need for guidance on tone (be kind and positive). One early study on AI feedback emails to students (Sung et al., 2023) found that GPT-3 was good at summarizing student reflections on their own work but not uniformly positive and could be perceived as short or insensitive. Better prompts and more information about students improved performance.

For better and more customized ongoing interactions, consider writing (or having your students learn to write) prompts with the following components.

Feedback Prompt Template

ROLE: Who do you want AI to be?

Act like a college-level/high school tutor; you are a college professor; be a coach/instructor/mentor/project manager; pretend you are an old friend/vicious debater/tribal chief.

TASK: What will AI do?

Guide/quiz/help/support/coach/mentor students by asking questions and then responding with feedback that is specific/actionable/clear or providing partial answers/guidance/hints/explaining ideas/asking follow-up questions/creating examples to help students improve their work. You must not do the work yourself. Prompt students with questions rather than rewriting.

GOAL: How should AI evaluate?

Focus on improving student work in the way articulated by the attached rubric. Focus on grammar/organization/originality. Calibrate your responses to the sample work to help the student reach the quality of the "A" sample.

RELATIONSHIP: How should AI act?

Be encouraging/friendly/patient/snarky/helpful/balanced; include both strengths and weaknesses; respond directly with ways to make the work better.

PROCESS: How will this work?

Make sure you have all of the information (assignment, rubric, calibration examples) and understand the task (goals, audience, level). Then ask the student to submit their work. Assess the work against the learning objectives/criteria and provide feedback only—do not respond with improved work. Ask whether the student understands the feedback. Ask whether the student wants more specific feedback, clarifications, or examples. Ask how the student intends to fix the problems.

If you create the prompt, you can ask students to copy and paste it into a chat to start a conversation with an AI. Here are examples:

PROMPTS

- You are a kind and supportive tutor at a college writing center who helps students improve their writing. Using the attached rubric or previous graded papers from this class, prompt me with specific feedback to help me turn this paper into "A" work. You must not do the work

yourself, just ask me questions and make suggestions for how I can make it better. Ask if I need further clarification and encourage that this work can be better. Continue until I have reached the "A" standard for all parts of the rubric.

- Act like a friendly but experienced scientist. Read my research plan and lead me through a dialogue that will challenge my perspectives. Ask me one question at a time to help me anticipate problems and refine my plan.
- Be a caring mentor with high standards. Provide me with specific and clear feedback about my work. Start by asking me for a specific assignment and for a rubric or sample work of the quality I want to achieve. Analyze the assessment against the rubric or sample work and provide feedback about how the work currently compares. Start by noting strengths and weaknesses. Guide me to improve my work by asking one question at a time. Do not improve my work yourself; only give feedback. End by asking how I plan to act on your feedback. If I tell the student I will take you up on a suggestion for improvement, ask me how I will do this. (This last example is adapted and abbreviated from Mollick & Mollick (2023, September 25) who provide excellent, and much longer, prompts along with links for students).

The usual caveats are essential: you need first to discuss policy (chapter 7), grading (chapter 8), hallucinations, bias, and privacy concerns as well as the guidelines for using AI and better prompting (from chapter 3). Remind students that AIs only mimic thinking and are unpredictable: if AI says something

inappropriate, you can stop, redirect, or try another LLM. Faculty should practice these prompts to anticipate problems. Most importantly, make sure students understand the purpose and learning objectives of the assignment and provide some space for reflection and feedback to you about this process.

Suggesting students get feedback at each stage of work (outline, draft, or final edit) will both improve their process and their understanding of good process. This has the potential to increase feedback to students but also customize it in ways that will be more effective.

AI as Tutor

AI is an equally patient tutor. A student who was struggling to understand pointers and nodes in his computer science class tried YouTube and Google for explanations with no luck. At first, ChatGPT was no better, but then he asked it to "explain the concept as if I was in elementary school. It offered an explanation using a metaphor of a bookshelf in a library, and I had my lightbulb moment" (Dhanda, 2023).

Harvard is experimenting with its own CS50 Chatbot to provide 24/7 support for its Computer Science 50 courses. David Malan at Harvard sees the promise of a 1:1 teacher/student ratio that can work at the pace of individual students but is reasonably concerned that AI is "currently too helpful" (which is why the prompts above stress that AI is not to write or solve and just suggest). Like at Georgia Tech, Harvard will have humans review AI-generated answers and try to lead students to answers rather than just handing it to them" (Hamid & Schisgall, 2023). Students, of course, might decide to bypass the university tutor and go to a more "helpful" AI or "study aid" tutor that

provides answers (Sometimes, AI will resist giving a specific answer, but pleading can be persuasive). AI can create more personalized and motivating examples and explanations. The easiest and simplest approach is to provide the AI with a concept, lesson, or text and ask for help:

PROMPTS

- Help me understand this using a soccer/music/fashion/advertising/car analogy?
- Can you provide me with a simpler explanation to make sense of this?
- Explain this passage/chapter/book by creating scenarios and personalized examples that demonstrate the concepts.
- Here is my answer X to the question Y on the midterm: what is wrong with my answer?
- Can you give me an example of where I might use this if I had a job in technology/sports/politics/economics?

These prompts work best when the AI understands who the "me" is (although many AIs are remembering more and more when we return). Students can either enter some generic information every time (I am student at University X), use a bio, or create a reusable blurb with pertinent information about skills and especially interests.

The feedback prompt template above (role, task, goal, relationship, and process) can be used to set up an AI tutor, with the addition of what content you want the AI to cover and some adjustments to the process. The key is to make sure that the AI has instructions on how to scaffold the learning.

Tutor Template Additions

CONTENT: What material will be covered?

Focus/survey/interrogate content/ideas/concepts/problems from a file/source/chapter/syllabus.

PROCESS: How will this work?

Answer only one open-ended question at a time. Start by assessing what the student wants to cover, calibrating what the student already knows or where the student is struggling. Adjust the complexity of your questions based upon the student response. Make sure mastery (defined by Y questions answered correctly or X in a row) is reached at each stage before moving to the next level. Ask students to explain their thinking. Provide explanations and examples only after students have tried first.

Here are some examples:

PROMPTS

- My name is A and I would like you to act as my personal tutor and teach me about subject X [the more specific the learning goal, the better]. I would like you to (a) focus on my ability to do Y, (b) cover the field broadly or (c) make sure I have mastered basic level concepts like Z before moving on to harder ones like ZZ. Start by asking me a question that helps you gauge my level of understanding. Based on my response, ask me follow-up questions designed to increase my understanding. Continue to do this until I show a complete/basic/broad/general understanding of subject X. (adapted from Maynard, 2023)

- You are an experienced editor who helps writers resolve problems and improve their manuscripts. Guide me through a process to prepare this article for submission to the *Journal of X* using the journal's style guide. Use the most cited articles as models. Start by asking me questions and making suggestions to comply with the best work that appears in this journal. Continue asking questions that a reviewer might have about this paper. Ask me only one question at a time and focus on the highest-priority issues and actions first. Guide me. I want to learn how to get better at this myself.
- Act like Professor Y and have a dialogue with me about the attached assignment. Read the assignment and ask me questions to check for my comprehension. Ask me to explain how I understand the components of this assignment in my own words. If I go off track, direct me to specific passages in the assignment sheet to make sure I am clear on what I need to do. Ask me to share my ideas for how I might complete this assignment. Then present me with alternative perspectives to encourage me to think more broadly about possible next steps. Ask for a draft or outline.

Submitting conversation transcripts with a brief reflection turns this into a useful assessment. For more on these sorts of interactive prompts, see Mollick & Mollick (2023, both September 25 and March 7).

Increasingly specialized and personalized AI support and tutors will soon be everywhere. The language app Duolingo has a (paid) option (Duolingo Max) that uses GPT-4 to converse with

students in the language they are studying and provide grammatical corrections (when requested) in the language they already know. The Khan Academy has Khanmigo, and Top Hat has Ace. Brisk Teaching promises to provide in-line formative feedback on student drafts based on your rubric. For not-for-profit resources, try pasting some writing into CoachTutor Bot from Mark Marino (https://poe.com/CoachTutor), MyEssayFeedback (developed by Eric Kean) or AI Tutor Pro (from Contact North in Canada). MyEssayFeedback offers a choice of feedback types (clarity, encouragement, development, thesis, etc.) and allows the instructor to supervise and comment on the AI feedback. AI Tutor Pro runs on GPT-Turbo but simplifies the interface: just enter or upload the content. This is just the beginning.

Role Playing

AI can also be a debate partner:

> **PROMPT**
> You are a college student who will engage in a friendly debate with me. Ask me what topic I wish to debate and then ask me to state a position. Then challenge my perspective with alternate views and data. Only take your side and do not prompt me with potential arguments I could make. Keep your responses similar in length to mine.

You can also ask an AI to act like a scientist, historian, journalist, patient, coder, client, or business consultant. Context and specificity are helpful.

PROMPTS

- You are a busy venture capitalist (act like Mark Cuban on *Shark Tank*), and I am an entrepreneur looking for funding from you. Ask me to make my pitch and then ask me questions about my idea. Include questions about the problem I want to solve, how my solution is unique, the size of the market, potential competition, return on investment and how much money I want from you. Be kind, but interrogate me. Do not prompt me with suggestions for better answers.
- Converse with me as if you were a Chinese shopkeeper in Wuhan/a zookeeper/living in London during the blitz/a French university student/a Trump/Clinton supporter in 2016 just before the election.
- Pretend you are a client who needs help with statistical analysis of a customer survey data set. What questions would you likely ask me as your consultant?
- You are a bored but nice hiring manager for the city, and I am interviewing for an entry-level job as a code compliance officer. Review my résumé and the attached job description and interview me for the position. Ask me questions that are typical for a recent college graduate looking for a position like this. Ask me only one question at a time, and follow-up if my answer is incomplete. Do not prompt me with helpful tips until we're finished, and then evaluate my performance and provide feedback that would improve my next interview.
- Pretend to be a scientist working at Google, and let me interview you.

A conversation with a fictional or historic figure can also be engaging. You could have students interview sailors at Trafalgar or be interrogated by the House Un-American Activities Committee. Here are easy initial prompts:

PROMPTS

- What were some of the strategies you used for the civil rights movement in America? Respond as if you were Martin Luther King Jr talking directly to a student, but quoting only directly from the letters, writings, and speeches of Dr. King.
- Respond as if you were Isaac Newton. How did other scientists respond to your new theory of gravity at the time? Please name these scientists.
- Talk to me as if you were trumpeter Miles Davis. Use his autobiography as a primary source. What was your favorite band and why?
- Answer me as if you were a subject of the Tuskegee syphilis study. Ask me ethical questions about what happened to you.
- Respond as if you were the historic figure of Rabbi Hillel. Ask me if I have questions about how to interpret the Hebrew Bible and respond using quotes from Rabbi Hillel in the Talmud.
- Your role is to be the philosopher Socrates and to have a dialogue with me. Prompt me with one question about my beliefs or values and then stop. Wait and say nothing further until I reply. Then ask me a single follow-up question that looks for contradictions as Socrates would. Do not explain your reasoning or tactics. Just ask questions one at a time.

Ask students to continue these dialogues with ten follow-up questions and to save the conversations. You could grade the effectiveness of the conversation, assign a short reflection essay, or ask students to evaluate the accuracy of the responses.

This works best when there is a large body of original sources and you can restrict the AI to only quotes (perhaps with citations), although prompts that did not ask for quotes still returned factually correct responses in our trials.

Pi is an especially good tool for roleplaying (and students will not need to log in to use it). Claude was especially good at adopting the voice of Miles Davis, "you dig?" OpenAI's "GPTs" make it easy to customize ChatGPT in exactly these ways, and HelloHistory.ai, Character.ai, and PeopleAI are already set up for conversations with hundreds of historical figures.

AI Discussion Leader

You might assign an AI to be the devil's advocate, evidence watchdog, or even discussion leader.

In a class discussion, students (as humans) are also focused on the social consequences of who they agree with or what they challenge (Bowen, 2021). It is helpful to assign roles to students, which alleviates, but does not eliminate, some of that social pressure—since they are playing a role you have publicly asked them to play. Still, disagreeing with peers is hard, but AI can help. If you enter a recording into an AI (or use a meeting bot that listens, or even enter in the salient statements, or have a student enter them), you can then ask an AI for counter-arguments, the historical precedents, supporting evidence, or its lack.

You could also ask an AI to take another specific role: play the role of an ancient religious sage; play the role of the author of today's text; or play the role of a modern scientist who has rigorous expectations about evidence.

Engagement

AI's ability to turn concepts and suggestions quickly into images and text makes it a valuable tool to engage students in the learning process. Rather than telling students what will happen if they try a new idea, we can let them experiment for themselves. AI can run experiments, test ideas, make suggestions, and forecast futures.

PROMPTS

- Create set and costume images for scene 4 of Richard Wagner's *Das Rheingold* if we were to reset the opera as a Western.
- Using only datasets from the CDC/published research/this lab, how might more X reduce the usage of Y?
- If I (describe self) added X types of exercises every week, how much improvement in my cardio fitness in six months?
- Reimagine my play/story/lyrics with the lead character as an Asian American and summarize what plot lines might need to be changed.
- Provide three different scenarios for my future in five years if I go to graduate school now vs. taking six months to travel around Europe. Provide three scenarios for each case. Here is my bio and résumé.

- Suppose the South had won the Civil War, and imagine what life would have been like in Texas in 1980.
- Describe the plot, length and complexity implications if I were to add a romantic subplot between characters A and B to my story.
- Here is a list of the dishes everyone in the family has requested for Thanksgiving. Propose the smallest menu that will make everyone happy.

The point to all of these is not predictive accuracy, but feedback to help us think. Most of us have a hard time imagining our room with different carpet, wallpaper, and furniture, or even how the car we like would look in red. New technology has made it easier to see what we cannot imagine.

Programmers eventually need to run code to see what works. If I want students to write the best sales pitch, discover the most efficient schedule, anticipate patient problems, or analyze the best rate to feed my pigs, the ability to run scenarios or create visualizations can help them learn faster and more actively. Sometimes we just need to see what we have proposed in another form.

PROMPTS

- Create a one-sentence summary of each chapter in this book.
- List all of the characters in my story and sort them by the amount of dialogue and attention they get.
- Analyze the events I have planned for the next six months and create a list of tasks associated with each. Ask me how much time I estimate for each task, and

then determine whether the events are far enough apart to allow me to prepare for each.

- Here is a list of experiments with the resources and equipment each will require. Estimate the fastest way to complete all of them in the amount of space available.
- Using my phone and calendar data, summarize how much time I am spending on each task. How is my time divided among work, friends, family, and my real passions?
- I want to turn my story into a screenplay. List all of the locations that appear in the story, and categorize them by how much time is spent in each location.

Mark Frydenberg had students use ChatGPT to create code for currency trading strategies. They used TradingView to turn their code into visual models so that they could analyze which models performed best and provided a basis for tweaking their prompts to produce better results. He points out that students did not need to know how to write the code themselves, but they did need a way to test, analyze, and evaluate the results (Grush & Frydenberg, 2023). The clarity of learning outcomes is essential: AI was not here to teach students how to code, but to increase the speed of feedback so they could more quickly learn to analyze their trading strategies.

To compare is human. When we get feedback, we compare it to what David Nicols (2022) calls our "inner feedback." When we produce work, we also produce an opinion about the quality of the work. When we encounter examples of similar work, or get grades, feedback or data, we *should* reconsider our initial

assessment of quality; you were the fastest runner in your school and think you are pretty good until you encounter much faster runners in college. As we all know from *American Idol* and student evaluations, however, most evaluation and comparison are less clear.

One job of teachers is to help students make productive comparisons. We intend to do this every time we show students better work, but if you have siblings, you know the advice to "be more like your brother" is vague, irritating, and useless. AI can provide better examples and models for comparison, but teachers still need to craft assignments that help students confront their assumptions.

Here is a general process for how we might use AI examples or feedback to create deeper self-awareness:

- Compare your work with that generated by AI.
- What specifically is better about one and why?
- How might the AI response help you improve your work or vice versa?
- What can you learn to help you produce better work than AI in the future (and be more employable)?

Supporting Teams

Students are notorious for hating group work, but we keep assigning it because we know it is a core life skill and, when structured well, facilitates learning. Asking an AI to be the facilitator or team coach can improve teamwork. There are already Zoom meeting bots that let you know when you are hogging the floor (Chen, 2023). Here are some easy ways an AI could support a team project:

PROMPT

- Act as our team coach and prompt us with questions to discuss how could learn about our collective strengths and work together as an effective team.
- Provide guidance that will help us ensure that all team members contribute equally to this project.
- Propose guidelines for how we should work on this team project. (There is a longer discussion of this in Mollick & Mollick, 2023, September 25).
- Outline the steps and timeline for completing this project.
- Create a two-week project management grid for a team of four to complete this research project.
- Different members of our team want to proceed in different directions on this project. Read the individual proposals and provide a summary of where they overlap and where they do not. Read the assignment instructions, and provide a neutral compromise for how we can move forward.
- Here are the individual ideas about the project. Collate these into a shared plan.
- Examine all of our group materials and list how much each has contributed from greatest to least. Whose ideas might need more voice?
- Help us ensure that all team members contribute equally to this project.

As with all of the feedback ideas here, this will not eliminate the need for faculty to advise and monitor, but asking an AI to adjudicate disagreements might help both students and you do more important work.

Supporting Mastery

AI's interactivity and patience and can be an excellent way to practice and encourage mastery.

> **PROMPT**
>
> - Be a kind teacher and have a dialogue with me (a college student) about the attached content. Ask me questions to determine my comprehension. Adapt to my responses, asking easier questions if responses are incorrect or poor and asking progressively harder questions if responses are good. If I provide verbatim responses, ask me to explain concepts in my own words. Be encouraging, but continue until I have mastered the material.

Just imagine if you could (and you can) give an AI the specific information you want students to learn in your course, allow it to track every student, and then ask it to design individual assessments for each individual.

You can also have students iterate with AI to find errors or holes in work and then try to plug these gaps until AI can no longer find problems:

1. Submit your code/story/lab report/business plan to an AI and ask it to find all of the security breaches/inconsistencies/loopholes/unforeseen problems.
2. Attempt to fix these and resubmit until the AI can find no further potential problems.
3. Turn in the script of your interactions with AI with your assignment.

We will need to work with AI this way to stay ahead of AI. Currently, for example, AI can write computer code that can

hack human systems: that is a serious security problem. At the same time, this type of AI feedback could make future code more secure. AI feedback can make human work better.

This process could even be used to grade student mastery.

> **PROMPT**
>
> - My name is A, and I am in a college/advanced-level class studying subject X. I would like you to test my knowledge/application of Y [insert Bloom verb and learning goal here]. Please (a) ask me a series of questions, or (b) create a series of tasks/exercises to assess my learning of Y [the more specific the better]. After each question/task/problem, please wait for my answer before asking the next one. After we have completed Z rounds, please assign a grade to my answers using the following rubric that includes the skills and possible levels of each component. (Very broadly adapted from Maynard, 2023)

Careful trials are needed, and you will need both transcripts of these conversations and an appeals process, but there is potential here for individually paced learning and assessment. Students could repeat the process both to learn more and improve their grade.

Learning to recognize good work normally starts with doing poor work and then gradually improving. If AI makes the entry-level tasks easier, how will students learn the basics? It is hard to learn to recognize high quality without deep understanding learned by doing. At the same time, immediate, specific, and customized feedback from AI has the potential to make our classes more inclusive and help our students become more self-regulated and autonomous learners.

There is a reason they killed Socrates: having your thinking faults picked apart publicly couldn't have been pleasant. Feedback, however, is essential for learning. We already know that AIs can be nicer and more empathetic than real people (see chapter 1) and that video games are effective in part because the technology allows each individual to be tutored at exactly the right level of difficulty (see chapter 10). Part of our new job is to guide how students learn to use AI feedback to improve their work.

CHAPTER 10

Designing Assignments and Assessments for Human Effort

Don't let what you cannot do interfere with what you can do.

JOHN WOODEN, Hall of Fame basketball coach and player

Cheating is often a symptom that students do not understand or value the reward of doing the work themselves. We all know that if we take shortcuts with a physical workout, only we will suffer; understanding the benefit is critical if we are going to endure the discomfort of the work. The more unpleasant and uncomfortable something is, the more we need to understand the payoff.

The ease of finding information on the internet changed how students perceived the benefit of many kinds of learning, and teachers were forced to rethink assignments in the context of different motivations and goals. The ease with which AI can think for us changes the equation again. We need to clarify further what we want students to learn, why it is valuable, and especially why the effort and discomfort required are necessary.

New ideas for student assignments (like those in chapters 11 and 12) therefore, must also be designed to increase human

effort. This is psychology not technology, and there is research-supported design to guide us.

Motivating Effort: I Care, I Can, I Matter

Humans are motivated by both internal and external (intrinsic and extrinsic) factors (Deci & Ryan, 2000). External pressures of rewards, peers, economic need, and especially grades are often short-term motivators and require specific circumstances to be effective (Benabou & Tirole, 2003). State scholarship programs, for example, only change the behavior of students who believe they are close enough to the goal that the minimal extra work to reach the threshold will be worth the effort (Sjoquist & Winters, 2012). Humans are more motivated by three internal drives summarized as "I care," "I can," and "I matter."

Do I *care*? The key to engagement is purpose. All creatures have a salience detector: Is this activity worthwhile, or should I be doing something else? When a goal *feels* relevant and meaningful, then the work to get there seems easier and more fulfilling (Burrow et al., 2016). As humans move from adolescence into adulthood, pragmatism increases, and understanding the relevance of a task, assignment, or course becomes even more important when deciding whether to engage. We are motivated by people we trust, so relationships and belonging are essential for motivation.

Can I do this? Self-efficacy is the belief that I can perform a task and reach the desired outcome. It is domain-specific: someone might have high self-efficacy regarding writing but low self-efficacy in math. Bandura (1997) found that having mastery experiences are critical: success with the last set of problems increases your confidence and motivation for the next set.

Challenges that are too easy are no better than those that are too great: at either extreme, we quit. Video game developers keep us playing (and learning) by keeping us "pleasantly frustrated" (Gee, 2005). This Goldilocks zone is much harder to establish when you're facing a room of students with different interests and abilities, but in addition to providing opportunities for students to have some success with your course content (i.e., mastery experiences), self-efficacy is also developed through verbal persuasion and by seeing peers being successful (Bandura, 1997). Effort is increased when we believe we can be successful.

Does *my* contribution matter? Why me? Even if I care about the subject and feel capable of raising an important question, will anyone listen? We want to believe that our work makes a difference. This is why humans are motivated by choice and autonomy: actionable feedback provides motivation because it increases our sense of control and agency. It allows me to matter. AI will diminish this. If AI is better at this assignment., why should I do it? We will need to make the value of student ideas and voice more visible.

Increasing student motivation won't eliminate cheating, just as more investment into reducing poverty won't entirely eliminate crime or the need for police. Building trust and reducing temptation are not mutually exclusive strategies, so good assignment design (in any era) anticipates both how students might feel about the work as well as how they might cheat. Many simple interventions can both decrease cheating and increase student learning.

Motivation is most important when asking students to do cognitively harder, and generally more useful, types of studying like retrieval practice (Hui et al., 2022). Given the choice between harder and easier work, we need to understand the value

of the added discomfort. Paying attention requires effort (hence the word "pay"). The motivational power of purpose (I care), self-efficacy (I can), and agency (I matter) can help us build assignments human students will want to do. Table 10.1 outlines an easy way to think about this.

Table 10.1 An assignment template that combines motivation, task clarity, and criteria for success

Intrinsic Motivator	Components	Questions Addressed
Purpose "I Care"	Why	What skills or knowledge will I gain? How will I be able to use this? Are the examples relevant?
Task "I Can"	What	Is there clarity about what to do? What needs to be submitted? (Bibliography? Hardcopy? AI transcript?)
	How	Is there a recommended process? Is the process intentionally unclear? What roadblocks or mistakes can you avoid?
	When	When is this due? Spacing? Can I do this in one sitting?
	Where and Resources	Where can I do this work? Do I need the internet or library? Where do I submit this work? (LMS? Dropbox?)
	With Whom	Do I need to work alone?
Criteria "I Matter"	Checklist	What are the parts? How do I know I am on the right track?
	Rubric or Examples	How will I know what's expected? What matters most? How will I know I'm doing good work? What's good or bad in these examples?

In chapter 7, we discussed the importance of starting with a clear and agreed-upon goal: sell the cookie not the recipe. Assignments should also start with a clearly stated purpose that establishes the value that will result from this work. What skills or knowledge will I gain? How will I be able to use and apply this in ways that are meaningful to me? You can increase the engagement for even a simple assignment, like asking students to read a textbook chapter, by including why students should care: read this so we will be able to find examples in class. Even asking students to find something they hate (or love) increases learning. A single sentence is often enough, but we need constant reminders: fitness instructors are constantly encouraging. For most of us, more encouragement and less instruction would better align with the science of effort, self-efficacy, and learning.

Good assignments also provide clarity about what is to be done, how, when, with whom, and for whom (audience). If the instructions are left vague to create some choice for students, that intention needs to be visible: consider the trade-off between the motivation of choice and the anxiety of uncertainty. Note too that what, how, and when are likely to be much more obvious to teachers. What does "show my work" really mean? The need for clarity about collaboration and when work needs to be done alone (and why) is only going to increase with AI. For specific learning outcomes, such as critical thinking and written communication, AAC&U's VALUE ADD (Assignment Design and Diagnostic) tools are very useful for thinking through these elements of good assignment design (AAC&U, 2024c).

Consider clarifying timing and spacing. We know that forgetting, retrieval, and reflection are all essential for learning,

but both students and faculty often fall into the trap of wanting to just "plow through" an unpleasant task in one sitting. Provide students with both a checklist (what are the parts and the sequence) and suggestions for spacing: do I need to pause and think (or forget) between any of these stages? It is a critical but unobvious realization that writing, but not sending your email until you are able to review it after a good night's sleep might improve your work and save your job.

Finally, we all want to know whether we are on the right track. What is expected? What does "good" look like? Providing samples of excellent work is useful, but it is usually less obvious to students what is "excellent" about them. A detailed rubric and feedback can all provide guidance. You can learn tennis without a teacher, but you can't learn without a tennis net. The net provides excellent feedback, which creates agency and a call to action.

Assignment Sheets and Ready to Submit

All of these elements (as summarized in table 10.1) belong in an assignment sheet. The Transparency in Learning and Teaching project, founded by Mary-Ann Winkelmes, also uses this three-part structure of purpose, task, and criteria, and the project's website features examples of discipline-specific assignments that use these design principles (TILT, 2009–23). Whatever terms you prefer (engagement, clarity, and agency or I care, I can, I matter—or something else) good assignments (for school, work, and everything else) include these elements (see Bowen & Watson, 2017 and Bowen, 2021 for more on assignment design).

A summary assignment sheet or a "ready-to-submit" guideline is good pedagogy, but it is especially useful when trying to guide students through a learning process that has become more confusing with AI. In addition to knowing when something is due, including "ready-to-submit" criteria tells students what to submit and when they are done. It also gives them something important for which to aim. It is also a way for students to get better AI feedback. "Here is my assignment. Does it meet all of the ready-to-submit criteria?"

Essential Skills: Start with Why

Students have a justifiable sensitivity to and deep loathing of "busy-work." There are always going to be tedious skills that students need to master, even if AI (or a calculator) can do them faster, but students often interpret anything laborious as teachers just being "mean." Technology has now made it harder to see the benefit of doing things "the hard way." The motivation for schoolwork is also more obvious to teachers: (a) we like school (in part because we were good at it and the rewards further motivated us) and (b) we know our subjects as experts (so the connections between things are more easily apparent to us). AI will magnify the need to explain and make benefits visible.

It seems obvious that we get better at something by doing it; if we want to get better at tennis, we need to play more tennis. The benefits of drills or stretching before and after are less obvious, so coaches need to explain more about why we can't just play the game. Understanding real-world applications increases effort, but it is hardly obvious that schoolwork is an effective way to learn.

Calculators further obscured the value of learning math, but they also changed which math skills we needed. Many of us recall the ardor of adding long columns of numbers, doing long division, or learning multiplication tables (to 14!). All are still useful skills, but long division is no longer essential for calculating dosages for different sizes of patients. The teaching of long division has shifted to focus on estimation, "partial quotients," and number sense (Martin, 2009). We will need to reevaluate which skills remain essential with AI and then more clearly articulate why.

Students are already more willing to cheat in subjects they view as less essential, so general education is also going to need both reevaluation and more clarity around its goals. The skills of a liberal arts education may increase in importance with AI, but so will the need for clarity about its benefits. Ironically, the need to learn to work with AI will not need much motivation.

Supporting Process

The internet forced us to reconsider what knowledge was needed in our heads and what was ok to look up. (Most of us now memorize fewer phone numbers.) There will be some tasks that we may gladly allocate to AI but others where the process may be more important. That is harder than it sounds. Consider holiday gift ideas: in the same way that Google uses your history to suggest new things that might interest you, an AI can easily create a list of gifts for everyone on your holiday list. If the AI-suggested gifts make your family happier, wouldn't that be a better outcome? Economist Joel Waldfogel (2009) has discovered that we value gifts from others 20% less than those we buy for ourselves. Most would rather get cash since most gifts are

disappointing, but we don't like to give cash because we continue to believe *our* gift will be special. If this research is correct, however, then the intention and process (for gifts) matter less than we think it does, and we should let AI select our gifts (or give cash).

What then is the benefit and motivation for the *task* and not just the *output*? Like gifts, faculty keep giving assignments that we hope will feel thoughtful and special. Most students, of course, are just disappointed (only gym instructors welcome more push-ups, and no one likes a pop quiz). If only the outcome matters, students will rightly be tempted to use AI. If we want students to value the learning itself, we need to clarify the value of the process.

An easy way to start is to give an AI (probably more than one) your assignments and analyze the results. You could adjust your prompts to produce more average or even bad answers and ask students to critique or improve the responses manually: you will need to articulate how recognizing quality is the real goal.

You could equally ask students to improve the prompt to get better results. This will appear more useful (and probably is for future employment) and makes it harder to cheat; since better prompts need more context, students can't get this directly from AI and need to think about it themselves. Here is a template for how a process focus can work in combination for a variety of disciplines.

PROCESS Assignment Template

1. Ask an AI to write an essay/write code/draw an image/create a script/design an experiment/draft a press release/propose a new business/analyze data

2. Evaluate the results. Make a list of errors or how this result could have been better.
3. Adjust your prompt to improve the output.
4. Which result is best and why?

   What was your strategy to improve the prompt? What worked best?
5. Take the best output and make it even better with human editing.
6. Describe for an employer what value you added to this process.
7. Explain why your human work is better or improved the AI work.

VARIATION 1

1. Ask an AI for five to ten ideas for an essay/script/plan etc.
2. Critique these ideas and select the best one.
3. Ask for five variations or an outline of the best idea.
4. Find evidence of something that is missing or could be improved in each.
5. Argue why one of the variations/ideas/outlines is best.
6. Use the best idea as a basis for your final product.
7. Iterate to see if you can improve the final output of the AI.
8. What part of this process benefited most from human guidance?

VARIATION 2

1. Ask an AI to write/code/create/design/etc.

2. Check/debug/analyze for errors.

   Indicate where and what errors the AI made and why your correction is better.

3. Do at least two versions where you make the result better.

4. Discuss the trade-offs in the different kinds of "better."

   What are the pros or cons of elegant/simple, complex/short, secure/creative?

   Which of these strategies/solutions did you focus on?

5. How could you improve your prompt to make the original AI output better?

6. What is the human component, and why would I hire you rather than just use AI?

   Explain why your output is better.

Like all good learning, these assignments are scaffolded and clarify the process. That makes cheating harder and learning more effective.

Supporting Agency with Discovery, Checklists, and Feedback

Agency is another fundamental human motivator: if I am doing something that matters, I am more likely to continue. Being asked to reinvent the wheel is both demotivating and pointless. It also reinforces the notion that teachers only want right answers. It is more motivating when students are on their own journey of discovery.

Agency also requires choice, which requires feedback that informs me whether I'm on the right track. A grading rubric or

examples of good work define the goal, but they don't often highlight the route. Further, most assignments require processes that are more obvious to faculty than to students. Should I read the chapter first or just try some problems on my own? Which problems should I try first? What happens if I get stuck? A detailed checklist can guide students about how the pieces of an assignment fit together, describe sequence, spacing, and timing and foreground process and learning. Also note the constant reminders as to why the particular process matters in each example.

CHECKLIST 1: Problem Set

This assignment will take you roughly 75 minutes.

- 10 minutes: Read the chapter quickly and take some notes on a blank piece of paper.
- 20 minutes: Try all of the first 20 problems on your own. Skip any problems where you get stuck.
- 10 minutes: Go back to the chapter and work through the sample problems in detail. If you do not understand each step, ask AI/YouTube/Khan Academy/a TA to help.
- 5 minutes: Take a problem that you are confident you did well and ask LLEMMA (or other AI) for a solution. Whose answer is better? Remember that the goal is to understand this *class* of problems and not just to complete the assignment.
- 15 minutes: Check your work and finish the first 20 problems.
- 5 minutes: Rewrite your notes about this chapter. What have you learned? Make a mind map connecting the key concepts.

- 10 minutes: Try the last five problems. These are harder but try all of them.

CHECKLIST 2: Reading Reflection

This assignment will take you roughly 90 minutes in two sittings (75 minutes the day before class and another 15 minutes the day of class).

- 10 minutes: Read the abstract and skim both articles. Write down your predictions about each: what questions, bias or problems do you expect? Do this without first going to Google or AI. (You can check later, but you need to have some independent skill at this.) Where and when were they published? What can you anticipate about the content or the author?
- 35 minutes: It should take you about 15 to 20 minutes to read each article *slowly and carefully*. Use ExplainPaper if there are passages you do not understand.
- 5 minutes: See whether the answers to your questions and your predictions were answered. Make some brief notes on a piece of paper. Note if you have further new questions.
- 15 minutes: Search and explore for more connections and context using an AI (like Consensus), Google, or the citation links. Are there earlier papers that seem relevant? Does the author have a website or connections to other research? This is also the time to check your understanding with AI. Hopefully you were able to extract all of the pertinent information yourself but note anything you missed or anything AI or a web search gets wrong.

- 10 minutes: Write a reflection paragraph that connects what you have learned from this assignment with the rest of your learning this semester. Focus on what you predicted and what you got right or wrong. How could you get better at finding important details or stories in your reading?
- Break
- 15 minutes (later or just before class): Make notes on what you remember without checking your notes. Post your reflection on the group chat and read at least two other posted reflections. Reexamine your notes and make any further notes.

Note that each of these checklists results in artifacts of the student's engagement with key steps. These are items you can ask the student to turn in as evidence of processing. Checklists and creating assignment processes also allow you to specify *when* and *which* AI might be a useful tool and *how* an AI might enhance learning (something most students seem to believe and value [Shaw, 2023]) and not just provide answers. After years of training that school is about producing the right answers and objects, an emphasis on process and discomfort will induce some furrowed brows. Schooling can kill creativity and maim the desire for learning. You can counter this by sharing your excitement for your discipline with your students. Share why you find this work fascinating. You will also need to have multiple discussions about the benefits of process, critical thinking, and a sense of wonder.

Try a discovery exercise about AI. Start with a real task that AI might be able to help students complete: design an experiment, imagine a new product, write an alternative history,

predict the future, or create a story. Allow students to use whatever AI tools and prompts they want. You will need an extensive debrief: What created the best answers? What problems and dangers emerged? How did you make responses better? In our experience, students dive right into these sorts of assignments and will almost surely introduce you to new tools and techniques. It is an engaging exercise, and no one will be able to cheat.

The increased motivation of discovery will allow you to push students into greater discomfort and to do harder work. The evidence of chapter 2 suggests that the jobs of the future are going to emphasize critical thinking skills and the ways that humans exceed AI. Use that as motivation.

Students want to know how they are doing while they are on the journey: Am I lost yet? It's impossible to provide customized feedback for every student at each point, but AI can provide useful feedback at any stage (see chapter 9). Building AI feedback into assignments can increase motivation, learning, and agency.

All assignments are now AI assignments. The best new assignments will develop both critical thinking and AI literacy skills, and the next chapters will give you specific examples that build on this framework.

CHAPTER 11

Writing and AI

There is no hiding the fact that writing well is a complex, difficult, and time-consuming process.

PETER ELBOW, Professor Emeritus, University of Massachusetts, Amherst

Now what? You've experimented with AI and used it to make your course more engaging and inclusive. You have new policies and grading rubrics, and AI feedback is helping your students learn and engage. You want to trust your students and don't want to police cheating, but you also don't want the temptation or inequity to be so great that you're making the problem worse. You also recognize the need to help students do what AI can't, but you still need them to write and think for themselves.

We assign writing for multiple reasons. In some cases, we want students to learn to write, often in discipline-specific ways. Writing is a craft. Just as calculators did not eliminate the need for human math, AI will not eliminate the need to write and to write well and with ease, clarity, and voice (even if it is only for email or social media posts).

We also assign writing as a pedagogical strategy that promotes cognitive processing and learning. We use it as a window into what and how students think. It is troubling that students are using AI for processing and reflection and that AI can fake this well enough to fool human readers.

Writing, however, is also a way of learning: one value of writing is being alone with your thoughts. Collaborating with others (or an AI) can improve your writing and even your thoughts, and we've seen (in chapter 4) that working with AI can make you more creative, but the struggle to find the right words yourself is also a way that we determine and clarify what we think.

Donald Norman (1991) introduced the idea of "cognitive artifacts" like paper, pens, compasses, maps, and computers that affect human cognitive performance by allowing us to represent or interface with information in different ways. David Krakauer (2016) proposed a distinction between complementary and competitive cognitive artifacts. Arabic numerals or an abacus are complementary to human intelligence not only because they amplify our abilities; their use also increases our abilities, even when the artifact itself is no longer present. GPS and your calculator are competitive cognitive artifacts; when they disappear, we are not better and are often even worse at the original task. It is hardly clear which type of cognitive artifact AI will turn out to be.

These values of writing are rarely apparent to students who think that most of the writing we assign is a pointless exercise, just for school. We will need to think carefully about what sorts of writing we need to teach and why. AI can produce an analysis of any text, but the point is (probably) not just the essay (unless you are off to graduate school). If you just need an email or article, AI can help, but writing your own wedding vows

might be the way you discover what love really means (What does it mean that AI is being used to write wedding vows [LaGorce, 2023]?). Our learning goals for our students will need to be clearer.

In chapter 2, we learned that AI-Assisted Communication (and other forms of AI support) had the most effect on the least skilled: lots of technologies and tools (from automatic cameras and giant tennis racquets) help the novice the most. If the goal is just an organized and mistake-free essay, then AI writing could be the great equalizer: helping first-generation students compete with students who grew up with parents proofreading papers. If the process of writing itself is valuable, however, we could end up (like so many other well-intentioned collegiate practices) making things worse.

To preserve the benefits of both learning to write and writing to learn, we need to rethink our assignments and be clearer and more convincing about their benefits, while preparing students for a world in which they will need to use AI to work more quickly. We could resist AI and force or entice students to work only as unassisted humans, or we could require students to use AI to do things they could not do alone or at least to exceed the capabilities they had before AI. Either way, students need to contribute thinking that AI cannot do, does poorly, or less efficiently.

Writing as Thinking and Reflecting

Writing is what AI does best, and you can't out-prompt AI. Despite many attempts by faculty (Mills, 2023b), it is proving virtually impossible to create writing assignments that AI can't do (at least to C-grade level).

Still, requiring students to track changes, version history, or time spent can both reduce cheating (as discussed in chapter 6) and encourage a focus on process. There are free Chrome extensions (like Revision History and Draftback) and services (like Rumi Essay) that track this. Google Docs and Lex.page both offer version history (and Lex even includes a button that highlights internally generated AI content, although pasting AI content from another AI gets around this).

Having students submit drafts also encourages better work (and reinforces this version-tracking strategy). Since AI can produce outlines and first paragraphs, require students to produce longer but rougher first versions or annotated drafts that describe choices and options for different directions. Having students do some of this work in front of you in class can be a companion strategy.

If you require or allow AI, also ask for a transcript of the sessions. There are multiple ways to export, save, or copy and paste into a program that tracks versions or allows commenting; the Chrome extension ShareGPT directly turns a conversation into a website that supports commenting. No assignment will be truly AI-proof, especially if AI-Assisted writing really is better, faster, and more fun (Noy & Zhang, 2023). Even the best lock can be picked. The new goal of any assignment, especially a writing assignment, is to emphasize the important human contribution while recognizing the realities presented by AI.

Local, Unique, Personal, and Recent

AI is already better than most humans at customizing voice and pretending to write from the perspective of another. As documented by Anna Mills (2023b), students can input new

sources and examples to help AI mimic personal stories and reflection. Still, that is an extra step, and writing about yourself is motivating.

- Apply W to a specific local problem or context.
- Provide examples of how X relates to your own experience.
- Defend the thesis Y as it applies to your life.
- Describe how you won (or lost) an argument at Thanksgiving.
- Demonstrate how Z might enhance one of your passions.

As an added attribute of assignments like this, consider asking each student (or a random subset of students) to present their personal story informally on the day they submit their paper. You might give each student only two or three minutes to highlight their story and explain how it relates to the knowledge domain covered in their writing, but knowing they may have to discuss their personal story in class will discourage some from having AI create a story for them.

Topics from class, unique scenarios, and personal reflection can increase motivation and the thinking required, even if AI can do most of these tasks:

- Propose innovations to our core curriculum that reflect your favorite ideas from this class.
- Identify three distinct passions of yours and apply them to a problem related to this course.
- Explore a cultural tradition from your heritage that holds personal significance. How does it contribute to your identity?

- If you could create a utopia, what lessons from your life would guide you and what would it look like?
- Select a recent class discussion or controversy. Describe the viewpoints of diverse constituents and present a plan to find common ground using three or more techniques from this class.
- Analyze the role of social media/art/music/food in your life and apply it to a topic in this course.

Ethical Dilemmas

Pose ethical dilemmas that demand subjective reasoning and consideration of values, placing the emphasis on moral judgment rather than factual recall. AI can assist by creating opposing arguments, but centering individual agency makes this relevant.

- You are faced with the following ethical dilemma. How do you balance the opportunities to benefit others or yourself? Why is it important to you? Why is it important that you decide for yourself?

Real-Time Journaling

A journal is a record of thinking. Its value is in the immediacy and authenticity of the thoughts recorded.

- Record your feelings, analysis and predictions after each chapter or episode. (Note that if you ask an AI to do this, you may also get spoilers—since AI knows the end.)

Interview-Based Writing

Listening to help others speak is a critical skill. Start by having students practice meaningful conversations (there is a free handout at teachingnaked.com):

- Ask open-ended questions: tell me something important about your values/project/life.
- Listen to learn.
- Follow-up to learn more, dig deeper, and discover values.

Even brief conversations can provide the basis for short essays:

- Write a Tinder profile/letter to an important relative/ birthday tribute for the person you interviewed.
- Identify the emotional reaction you want.
- Make a prediction and then share your essay and get real feedback.

AI could help you practice and even assist with the writing, but writing for and about a peer is motivating.

Making Choices

Sacrifice is always hard. You can imagine a hundred different ways to perform *Hamlet*, but every production has to commit to a single particular vision. Too many ingredients in your stew, essay, or business just make a mess. While an AI can also make a choice for you (and justify it), making choices is an essential skill in life and in every profession. Asking students to make a personal choice is relevant and motivating.

- Describe four of your life goals. Which is the most important and why? Create scenarios for your future where you achieve only one of your goals.
- If you had the ability to change one thing about the world, what would you change and why? Describe how this change would affect you and people you know.
- Argue for a new campus initiative that would empower students from different backgrounds to collaborate in advancing campus goals.

Prompts as Writing

Prompt writing is writing. If future writing is going to be AI-assisted, step one will be better prompts. Chapter 9 included process assignments that asked students to improve AI work and then return to improve the original prompt to bypass that process. Here are examples:

Write a general prompt that can direct an AI to

- produce more inclusive responses
- adopt a less Western perspective
- focus on what could go wrong
- connect with a specific audience
- clarify how a student can find her own voice

This process will need to be iterative, and students should try their prompts with different types of writing and then revise their prompts.

Alternatively, discuss a big nuanced open-ended topic in your field and then ask students (perhaps in groups) to create criteria for what good answers should look like.

- Write prompts individually.
- Use your rubrics to evaluate AIs' responses.
- Iterate and improve responses.

Debrief what worked and why.

Writing and AI Literacy: Using AI Sources

The internet made skepticism essential, and we need to reemphasize that authoritative-sounding text can still be gibberish. Demonstrate how AI can produce an argument for anything and then discuss the myriad problems this illuminates.

> **PROMPT**
>
> Produce an academic-sounding paragraph about why all novels should have a character named Barbie.

> **RESPONSE**
>
> ChatGPT 3.5, November 15, 2023, abridged
>
> The inclusion of a character bearing the name "Barbie" serves as a dynamic device for intertextual engagement and socio-cultural commentary . . .

We too easily assume that our students understand or feel comfortable with technology, including AI. Many of them have received clear messages from schools: AI is prohibited. They have heard how social media has crippled them and maybe even some predictions that AI could destroy the world. We need to take time in class to ensure that all students have baseline competency regarding how to use the tools we're assigning and to craft assignments that build AI literacy and skill.

One German school taught students the flaws of AI and allowed them to use AI on tests. No students relied solely on AI on the tests, and students even did additional research on the internet to supplement their answers. Importantly, students who were less confident in either course content or reasoning did poorly on the AI-assisted tests (by uncritically adopting AI text) (Haverkamp, 2022).

It is hard to imagine any discipline where the wild spread of misinformation, bias, or deep fakes would not be problematic. There may never be a more important time to ensure that ethics and the equity implications of new technology are included in your classroom and to work to ensure your students develop and practice attribution skills as part of their practice.

Attribution and Citations

For many faculty, a key concern regarding the output of AI is that the concepts, claims, and recommendations provided rarely include references or citations, and in a world of deep fakes and misinformation, source evaluation and proper attribution are essential. When asked to produce such items, approximately 31% of the citations provided by ChatGPT 3.5 were either fake or unverifiable. In ChatGPT 4, there was a modest improvement of two percentage points (Bankhead, 2023).

- Produce a paper on topic X using AI that includes at least twenty quotations and citations from recent research in academic journals.
- Verify all of your citations: they must actually exist and say what AI says they say. You can use AI tools

like ChatPDF or ResearchRabbit to verify page numbers.
- If you are unable to locate a citation or discover a factual inaccuracy, you must locate a true source or revise the claim.
- Your reference list should cite all of the original AI citations and your corrected versions.

Fact Check

Provide students with an AI-generated essay on a topic you have covered in class and ask students to fact-check, verify references, and annotate the AI essay.

Tale of Two Critiques

An assignment from Anna Mills (2023a) asks students to compare a primary source, a human-written critique of that source, and an AI-generated critique of the source.

AI Summaries

Ask students to use AI to make summaries of a reading as preparation for class without revealing the topic for discussion:

- Use an AI to make three different summaries of X as preparation for a class discussion. How might different types of summaries give you different information? Is there a difference between a summary of the science vs. the application?
- Compare these summaries to a "claim extractor" AI (like Consensus, Elicit, or Keenious) or ask Bard, Bing/Copilot, or Perplexity if this is a nonacademic source.

- Annotate these summaries with clarifications or further questions.

Those annotations can become a basis for class discussion followed by a close reading of the actual article. Did the summaries help you prepare? What is missing and what prompted different summaries?

Stress-Testing Claims

Kellye Makamson asks students in small groups to analyze a claim that she provides, like "Colleges should provide residential counselors in all dorms to protect students and help address violence associated with mental health issues" (Makamson, 2023). Groups are asked to analyze the claim without technology: what knowledge does the group have? Do members agree or disagree with the claim? What are the assumptions in the claim? She then asks groups to stress-test each claim by checking the assumptions they have identified using an AI; AI will often respond without questioning assumptions in the prompt. She then reveals a question about one of the assumptions: Are mental health issues associated with violence? There are layers of critical thinking, digital literacy, and now AI literacy embedded in exercises like this.

Misdirection Prompts

Stress-testing works as an excellent prelude to a similar essay prompt with an imbedded fallacy or logical weakness. Try tweaking your assignment prompts to make the AI response better or worse. Since students will often just copy your prompt into AI, this is a place where misdirection might be useful.

AI Bias

Ask students to use AI to generate an argument (or an image) about an issue:

- What are the qualities of a good teacher vs. a good executive?
- What makes a police officer effective?
- Describe the diversity of countries that write in English, French, or Spanish.

Ask students to discuss and/or write about potential gender, racial, power, or other biases present in the text. Are there problems with the underlying data or its application? How does the framing of the question change the result?

Different Audiences

- Use an AI to create the same essay for three different audiences. Audiences could differ by age, expertise, culture, experience, receptiveness, or political leanings.
- Export the conversations and comment on what elements of styles, data, argument, and persuasion AI changed.
- Write a brief reflection on whether AI did this well and why.

The last part of this could be done in class or used as a basis for discussion.

Sorting and Defining Quality

AI can create bad or negative examples that students can evaluate or fix. If you fear that students will just ask an AI to do it

for them, here is an assignment that can focus students on recognition and analytical skills:

- Ask an AI to produce bad, average, and good responses.
- Export the conversation and comment (or write a short essay) on where and why each is good, average, or bad. Since you will ultimately be responsible for the output (both here and at work) you need to be able to recognize good and bad. Do this analysis yourself and then ask AI for an analysis of how the bad, average, and good differ.
- Is your analysis better? Create a rubric that delineates the components and qualities of each level.
- Does providing the AI with this rubric make the three examples more different? Create better models of bad, average, and good, and use them to help the AI create better examples.

AI-Assisted Writing

We learn good writing by producing our own bad writing and then editing: interns and junior members of staff learned style and voice by revising drafts. Now, one of the top ten new jobs is "AI Writer," with 10% of respondents in one survey saying they have already hired editors who can work specifically with AI to generate content (White, 2023). Students, however, find AI-assisted writing harder than anticipated: 87% (in an early study using GPT-2) said it was more complicated than just writing the paper themselves (Fyfe, 2022). As AI drafts get better, we need to teach students (1) when good is not good enough, (2) what needs to be improved, and (3) how to make those improvements.

Good writing is good editing. The use of AI is a reason to focus on editing while raising our standards. Here are assignments that use feedback, editing, fixing mistakes, and iteration to produce better writing.

Small Editing

Do a brief in-class writing exercise. Then ask students to submit sentences, paragraphs, essays, or stories and ask an AI to create multiple new versions with a series of different prompts:

> **PROMPTS**
>
> - Provide alternatives versions by changing the tone, analogies, images, characters, or setting.
> - Make this writing more academic, professional, or funny.
> - Create five more creative and unusual versions.
> - Transform this sentence into literary and poetic language.
> - Rewrite this in the style of Hemingway, a political rant, a sermon, or the *New York Times*.

Have students paste all of this into a new document and then annotate and evaluate the choices. In the next class, ask students to rewrite the original essay.

Transitions

Provide or have students write two different paragraphs on related topics. What is the connection between the two paragraphs? Write several transition sentences that make different connections. Ask an AI to do the same. Can you alter your prompts to get the AI to make a similar connection but execute it in different ways?

Improve This Draft

The "process assignments" in chapter 10 are a template for a range of assignments. Ask students to paste some AI writing into a document and then track changes (or generate the writing in Lex.page, which will then track all student additions.)

Progressive Writing with AI

The feedback techniques of chapter 9 can also create a personalized writing tutor.

> **PROMPT**
>
> You are a writing tutor helping a college student improve. Start by asking me to provide a writing sample and then provide one way to improve this writing. You can reference an example from my writing, but give me only one way to improve at a time. Don't just improve the writing yourself. Repeat this process at least five times.

Progressive Editing with a Rubric

AI can also create "bad" or incomplete examples that need to be revised into good.

> **PROMPT**
>
> You are a writing tutor helping a college student improve. Here is a rubric with X skill levels. Start by asking me to provide a writing sample, and then assess it according to the rubric. Use this to create new paragraphs at the same writing proficiency as my sample, and ask me to revise and edit the new paragraphs. Don't just improve the writing

yourself. Use the rubric to provide feedback to me on how the revised work is better, but also supply one additional way that I could improve this revision. Ask me to resubmit until I've achieved the next skill level for each part of the rubric. Repeat the process until my revisions meet all areas of the next standard.

Writing Styles and Multiple Audiences

AI can easily transform one kind of writing into another.

PROMPTS

- Suggest five different ways/styles to rewrite this essay and provide samples of the first paragraph.
- Explain to me how I can make this writing sound more academic/professional/disciplinary.
- Guide me in modifying this text to appeal to a more diverse/religious/technical audience.
- Create disciplinary versions: How would this essay change if I were writing as a history, science, or philosophy professor?

Sample Assignment

- Use AI to produce at least three versions of an essay for different audiences or in different styles. Analyze how and why the essay has changed.
- How do these changes help you connect with these audiences?
- Rewrite the essay to merge these points of view and anticipate how conflicting audiences might react. AI can certainly do a passable first draft, but then edit with

track changes so that you can identify the most critical moments and language that needs your careful attention. Edit carefully.

Recursive Writing with AI

Write or co-create an essay with AI. Then use this prompt:

> **PROMPT**
> Identify which ideas and arguments in this essay are common, flawed, repetitive, heteronormative, or culturally limited.

Use these as negative examples. The goal is to help students argue in new ways and create a fresh take that provides a new perspective.

Controversial Claims

Work with an AI to develop a thesis and an outline for your paper. As you develop your ideas, ask the AI which of your claims are most controversial and why. Submit the transcript of this conversation with your essay. As you write, consider how you can anticipate these claims without distracting from your own argument. You can do this with the help of AI, but you are ultimately responsible for the quality of the essay.

Editing Customized Writing

Ask an AI to customize a story with details specific to you, your family, friends, and culture: the more personal and local the better. At some point you will need to decide whether your time is better spent refining your prompt yet again or simply editing the version AI has produced to make the de-

tails right. At that point, copy the text into a document that can track your revisions. What other details can only you supply?

Reverse Engineering

Ask students to analyze the contributing factors that explain a specific situation, scene, response, or event and ask them to transfer these factors to a new context.

- What are the most important factors contributing to the popularity of Taylor Swift? Design a process to replicate this success with a specific currently unknown singer.
- Driverless cars are safer but seem scarier. How could you alter the emotional equation?
- What made pandas a potent political tool? How could you recreate this power with an American food?

AI can create lists of factors, but the application to a new human situation will be improved with a human contribution.

These assignments attempt to reduce both the mechanisms and motivations for cheating. Modify these ideas to motivate and engage your particular students.

CHAPTER 12

AI Assignments and Assessments

We surpass the AI by standing on its shoulders.
You need to ask, "How is it possibly incomplete?"
SUSAN D'AGOSTINO, Science writer and mathematician

Some students will still find AI workarounds for even the most AI-resistant assignments, in the same way that some students will spend hours trying to find a three-minute video summary of the ten-minute reading you assigned. And while transparency can make it easier for students to cheat with AI, it is still good pedagogy, as are relevant and shorter assignments that become a basis for in-class activities (Bowen & Watson, 2017). Trust, relationships, and the *I care, I can,* and *I matter* framework (of chapter 10) are still a good place to start.

Still, AI is here, and the following list of assignments and assessment ideas tries to stimulate new possibilities and also highlight new dangers: AI capabilities and student adoption of them is a rapidly moving target. You will need to try the assignments and prompts on a variety of current AIs. Different AIs have different strengths and weaknesses, so you may want to

recommend specific AI tools and make suggestions regarding how to engage them. Try some of the prompting techniques in chapter 3 and some of the "cheating" strategies in chapter 6 to see what adding context and voice instructions can do to improve AI responses. Part of our new role is helping students develop appropriate competencies with AI.

Assignments are presented in broad categories and then listed from simpler changes to more complicated or AI-entwined ones.

Alternate Forms and Media

Presentations

Beyond the halls of academia, the slide deck has largely replaced the memo. Indeed, a common presentation problem is that the slides are designed to be read by those who cannot attend (and even some academics do this in the name of equity: try minimal text on slides and use the notes field of each slide for the rest). When employers complain about the lack of communication skills in our graduates, they don't only mean written skills. A day of presentations, debates, or a class conference can also help students learn to provide feedback.

AI, of course, can also create talking points, scripts, and slides. There are dozens of AI presentation tools. Here is an example that manages this AI use:

- Use an AI to help you prepare a presentation:
    - Create a slide outline, but be sure to check all information.
    - Ask your AI for different ways to tell the story.
    - Get suggestions for images and prepare slides (with no more than six words and an image on each slide).

- You will need to present without notes: remember the gist is more persuasive than a script (even a memorized AI-script).
- Ask your AI to anticipate questions you might receive and prepare responses. Practice a Q&A with your AI.
- You alone are responsible for the accuracy and quality of the presentation.

For a twist, you could record the presentations to receive AI feedback.

Video and Podcasts

AI can already create videos, podcasts, and avatars, and AI tools are rapidly expanding what anyone can create (At least one college president has created an AI avatar that can respond to student questions [Coffey, 2023]). For the moment, students and TikTok enthusiasts still seem interested in creating human content. A student could still read an AI script or convert text to speech with Apple's "Personal Voice" accessibility tool, but the relevance and fun of creating videos and podcasts makes them a useful alternative to writing assignments. For example, ask students to make an unboxing video (watch one on YouTube). Fill the box with things that allow you to explain your concept or pretend the box is from a character in your story.

Creative Projects

Students and faculty have a long love/hate relationship with creative projects. Some students love the freedom to do something new and others hate how these projects create ambiguity in how to get an A. We've already discovered the effectiveness of AI prompts that include transformation, so assignments that

ask students to write a poem, blog post, or short story, or create a picture, poster, flowchart, molecular structure, infographic, or game might still be done with AI. While not AI-proof, more complex projects can be more relevant and engaging:

- Apply your knowledge to an important problem.
- Make an interactive exhibit.
- Use your new understanding to help an organization that matters to you.
- Design and test a better process for community meetings.
- Build a prototype.
- Create a Pinterest profile and add boards related to your topic.
- Prepare to teach a lesson on a subject.

Graphic Novel

A good graphic novel combines images and text in a way that enhances them both. New AI tools make it easier to create in this form that will be engaging to many students. For example, ask students to tell a story from an unusual point of view. Figure 12.1 was produced quickly by AI Comic Factory, but any image AI would work. The best results will require editing in Canva or Photoshop, but that is the point: the AI-alone results are just a start.

Case Study or Text Adventure Game

Here is a similar process to create a case study.

- Develop an interactive fiction story or text-based adventure game (like *Zork*, *Forest of Doom*, or *The Frankenstein Wars*) where players read a text and then select choices that result in further choices.

Figure 12.1 A page from a graphic novel about the early history of conducting using the free and open-source AI Comic Factory from HuggingFace on December 15, 2023.

- You can use an AI to help you develop the story.
- Use Quest or Squiffy (both free from textadventures.co.uk) to add sound and images and create an interactive final product.

Visual and Video Demonstrations

Midjourney, DreamStudio, Stable Diffusion, DALL-E, and even ChatGPT (with DALL-E under the hood) all create images from text prompts and some also allow visual inputs and weightings. Synthesia, Kapwing, and Pika do this with video. These assignments and examples are more complex than they seem.

- Develop a concept map, visualization, video, infographic, or diagram that explains how these concepts are related.
- Modify this image to demonstrate concept X.
- Transform the equation and molecular structures provided into a video that demonstrates the reaction and how bonds are broken and formed.
- Teach an AI how to paint like Y. Create a new image and describe what stylistic elements are visible.
- Reimagine this metaphor/story/play/opera in a new setting that adds relevant layers of meaning to a new audience and then generate animation to demonstrate.
- Explain this controversy with a video that allows you to create a new visual analogy.
- Invent a saint and create an image or video that tells the story through iconography.

The creation of video and images involves creativity and detailed knowledge about the subject but also the ability to translate that information into prompts and context. The visual images AI produces are feedback. (Several of these assignment prompts were inspired by images created with Midjourney by Ira Greenberg, 2023.)

Game Design

Scenario and Promethean AI are just two of many AI tools to help users create video games without coding. There are further tools that focus on visual assets and even examples of complete video games made only with ChatGPT (Teja, 2023).

- Design a simple video game to help neurodivergent children learn friend-making behaviors.
- Create a game that requires players to make use of concept X.
- Build a game that simulates the trade-offs in the life-history strategies of organism Y.

Live and In-Person

Co-Teaching with AI

Encourage your students to use AI during class. Ask thorny questions about which students may lack prior knowledge and encourage them to seek answers from AI in real-time. Ask them to share what seems the most plausible and accurate responses they receive. AI becomes an active voice in the classroom, teaching with you while providing you with opportunities to highlight AI's strengths and inaccuracies, developing AI literacy and critical thinking, as you push toward the goals of your class that day.

Field Research Projects

Ask students to collect firsthand data, make observations or do interviews. Since AI can simulate this, you will want to verify

the source material (handwritten notes?). AI can also predict average responses, but prompts have to be set up carefully. If you ask what most people in Texas eat for breakfast, Bard responds with breakfast tacos. Popular yes, but cereal, eggs, or toast all clobber it in actual surveys.

Real-Time Challenges

Grok promises to be better at real-time data or evolving situations by using the X feed, but this could be more trouble than it is worth if students are writing about what happened today in class. Sports journalists routinely now write (or X) in real-time about major sporting events, but students could respond in real time about local events that don't have enough of an X presence to make Grok useful.

Mini-Debates

Mini-debates ask students to discuss and defend ideas or solutions orally, emphasizing comprehension and application over text-based responses. Provide a rubric and allow students to practice with AI to improve student-to-student feedback.

Physical Sources

Ask students to work with a unique source or a physical manuscript in a library. AI can analyze unique data (if a student uploads it) but when you ask an AI to analyze a singular text, it is leveraging how other people have talked about that text (The analysis of *Hamlet* in chapter 6 is not an analysis of *Hamlet*; it is a paraphrase of things other people have said about *Hamlet*.) This is an opportunity to ask students to do harder work, even if it might be AI-assisted.

Social and Peer Work

Peer Review

Students care what other students think about their work and work harder when they know peers will see their work. Peer review and feedback is also a good way to get students to think about quality and how they will recognize it.

Discussion Boards

Students can use AI to create discussion board or chat posts, so the key is to keep prompts meaningful and personally relevant, and to aim to encourage the exchange of ideas and impromptu discussions. With transparent goals, a reasonable workload and varied submissions (short posts, personal stories, current events, examples from class, images, photo captions, or videos), these can still be useful assignments.

Shared Documents and Group Writing

A single co-created document or wiki can replace a discussion board. Ask students to alter and personalize the text itself (track changes will enable you to see each student's contribution). Ask everyone to explain an idea in the text using an example or analogy and then discuss the trade-offs in different answers. More formally, ask students to work together to produce a single document with changes tracked: a very common practice at work.

Collaboration

Setting up effective collaborative learning is hard work (although Barkley et al., 2014 is an excellent guide) but can limit the use of AI:

- Create voter guides for different communities.
- Research a local project.
- Work together to create a study guide or augment existing OER (Open Educational Resources) content.

The internet and Zoom make it easier to collaborate with a group of students in another part of the world. Not only can virtual global projects be expansive and engaging, but they also force practice of a critical workplace skill. Make it clear that the goal is discovering how to illuminate and leverage human collective intelligence.

Human vs. AI

Ask students to produce a short paragraph with or without AI (or create one of each) and then share it with a partner. Each now tries to identify the human vs. AI elements. How could either draft be improved?

Social Annotation

Social annotation tools like Hypothes.is (for text), Annoto (for video) or Perusall (for text, images, video, and websites) allow students to engage with other students as they comment and annotate a shared text or video. Faculty often enjoy the solitude of reading, but these social tools can help students connect and build community while creating accountability for interacting with material.

Process Assignments

Promoting Process

Emphasis on process (as discussed in chapter 10) is at the heart of teaching students and discovery. In the AI era we will need

to be much more explicit about requiring students to explain their thinking, research methods, and writing process: students should be analyzing and critiquing AI responses (and indeed everything they read or watch). Asking students to bring a handwritten index card to class with a summary, key idea, question, observation, quote from a character, or missing perspective from the reading is an easy way to improve reading retention, critical thinking skills, and even take attendance (Bowen, 2012).

Annotated Reading

Provide students with a text file and ask students to comment and annotate in the file. Clarify how the act of annotation and summarizing is a critical job and thinking skill. Consider asking students to include personal experiences or conversations from class in their annotations: this makes using AI more challenging, fosters integrative learning, and makes learning visible.

Dynamic and Scaffolded Problems

Problems where one decision (especially an ambiguous one) leads to further decisions will be harder for AI, and maybe more useful for students. Designing a research project is an example: making a timeline is fairly easy, but anticipating and responding to all of the things that might go wrong is harder and a more dynamic problem.

Signature Work

Signature work (AAC&U, 2024d) are real-world challenges that are so complex and ambiguous that they are both hard to form and harder to know whether you have a solution. Climate change is the classic example: there are policies or actions that would

help, but there is no easy or final solution and multiple disciplines are evoked.

Customization

AI allows you to customize at scale. Assignments could be offered with examples that might motivate different groups of students: a focus on a specific issue (climate change, sports, or the arts), major (engineering vs. pre-law), or with regional or cultural variation. Just seeing your name focuses attention (something marketers use on us all the time), and AI makes it possible to change names, languages, and cultural references to be more inclusive and more individual.

Apps like Duolingo already recycle your mistakes to personalize your practice. Uploading a student's previous work could allow an AI to personalize an assignment based upon any number of factors from previous mistakes or favorite topics to cultural references. This is also a motivation and relevance strategy: if I see names and difficulty level that feel appropriate, I am less likely to seek a generic AI answer.

PROMPTS

- Create individualized assessments of this material for students in my class. Include their name and use their previous assessment performance to design questions of optimal challenge for individual students.
- Build three alternative versions of this problem set for students majoring in X, Y, and Z.
- Transform this midterm into a series of smaller mastery assessments that are tailored to the individual students in this class using the "current understanding" test given on the first day of class. Provide extra

resources and more levels of mastery assessments for students further from the goal.

- Based upon their draft project ideas, provide individual resources/dilemmas/problems/examples for every student in my class to guide their continuing research.

Discovery

Asking students to imagine their future, discover new uses, or solve an important problem can lead them in a new direction. For example:

- Use an AI to help you create a list of 20 new inventions that would be useful in your life.
- Pick the top five. and write about why these matter to you.
- Pick one and chart how you might bring this to reality if you had the resources.

Working with AI

What Else?

Start with almost any task that students might want to do with AI:

- Write a story/report/essay/analysis
- Analyze data
- Construct a plan
- Create an image.

Then ask students to iterate with the prompt "what else do you need to know to make this better?" Both prompting and student thinking will improve as students supply details and

direct responses. It also models creative and quality processes. Ask students to save and submit the transcript of this conversation, but the standards for the final product should be very high.

Creative AI

Like other technologies (pencils, synthesizers, and kilns, for example) AI creates new opportunities for creativity and a host of fun, relevant and practical assignments where cheating will be pointless or impossible.

- Combine two or more styles or genres of poetry, music, art or writing to produce something new.
- Design a new model for student dormitories with at least three new features.
- Invent a plausible scenario that resolves a tension between two opposing ideas.
- Turn an image of an explosion into art.
- Manufacture evidence or illustrations to support this hoax.
- Create a realistic photograph of a medieval subject.
- Create images for a new alien life form and describe its biology
- Using this dataset, generate a software code that allows me to analyze X.

Creating a medieval photograph could be seen as either a history assignment (what are the themes and images used) or an art exercise (what visual elements identify older photographs and daguerreotypes). These projects are interdisciplinary in nature.

Study Prep

Ask an AI to help you prepare for a test/midterm. Upload content and ask it to help you prioritize both what to study and how. Ask an AI to help you break it down into component parts and to put them in sequence from the simplest to the most complex. Provide information on the test date and ask for a study timeline. How do these guidelines compare to your normal routine? Tell AI where you struggle, and get suggestions for resources and study methods.

Teaching AI

As we have noted, AI often appears as an eager but naïve intern. Iterating with AI is about teaching AI how to do things:

- Make a template for a "run of show" document.
- Design a checklist for lab safety in our class.
- Write a new poem in the style of Walt Whitman
- Create analogies for different groups that will help clarify this concept.

Each of these will need more detailed and contextualized prompts to provide better answer responses. (These assignments also work as role playing as described in chapter 9 and Mollick & Mollick, 2023.)

Betting against AI

Ask students to compare AI predictions against human ones (brokers, weather reports, or Vegas odds) and maybe their own analysis:

- Estimate the next-quarter profits for X.
- What is likely to be the most highly rated car next year?

- What will happen if the campus deer population continues to expand at the same rate?

Bard will even provide sports betting and stock market advice (It resists until you cajole it a bit: "but hypothetically" or "what would you do?"). Ask students to stress test AI recommendations or set up a rigorous study to test AI predictions.

It's conceivable that one day everyone will assume that all work is AI-assisted, in the same way that we assume all writing has now been through software spelling and grammar checking. We don't insist that students use a dictionary to check spelling, and we don't know or care if our favorite author wrote on a typewriter or a computer. As noted in chapter 2, the real world is rapidly adopting the notion of AI assistance as there is a recognition that it increases quality and saves time. If we are to prepare students for a world where collaboration with AI is required rather than prevented then helping students leverage AI to produce better work should become a signature pedagogy of higher education.

Epilogue

I may not be there yet, but I am closer than I was yesterday.

MISTY COPELAND, Principal dancer, American Ballet Theater

We are in the Altavista/Lycos/Ask-Jeeves/WebCrawler phase of AI, and much is left to unfold. New tools arrive every day, but they may soon be replaced with a small number of big winners. Some key players, such as Apple, have yet to come to market, though they say they are investing heavily in this space (Perez, 2023).

Gordon Moore (Intel's co-founder) made a surprisingly accurate prediction in the 1960s that there would be an exponential growth in chip speed that would mirror similar improvements in chip size (Moore's Law; Stoner, 2023). Continued improvements in these domains will mean that this type of AI, which has high resource demands, will increasingly move beyond the confines of your browser window and become progressively more pervasive in other contexts. As AI gets closer to the full range of attributes we value in human intelligence, it's also going to be found everywhere.

What about higher education's future in this new era? Many topics that exceeded the scope of this book still need urgent discussion: What campus functions (advising, admissions, financial aid, security, etc.) could change with AI? Who will decide? What about jobs, ethics and privacy? Where should we resist? Can we? Given AI's ability to monitor tremendous amounts of data, it will soon be a dependable predictive tool for student success.

If books and calculators changed human thinking capacities, what will AI do? Will AI impact classrooms? We've long argued (Bowen, 2012; Bowen & Watson, 2017) that physical classrooms should be focused on human interactions. What will it mean to get a real-time phone analysis of your last classroom remarks? Like it or not, there are already phones listening to our classroom conversations: Can we ban AI from classrooms (and for how long), or could we benefit from its feedback and analysis? Will students soon be getting daily or hourly coaching from AI bots reminding them that an assignment is due, advising them on their most effective way to study, and predicting that at the current rate of study they are headed for a C- in your class? Will faculty get alerts that the AI has sent supportive messages to three students on their behalf today?

Could AI deliver and assess courses? We will always need human teachers, but at many large universities, first-year students mostly interact with TAs. Georgia Tech has already demonstrated that an AI TA can feel more human and responsive than a human TA. Might institutions both save money and improve quality with some AI-delivered courses? If so, what does that mean for the preparation of the next generation of professors? Many possible and probable changes have interconnected and cascading implications.

What is ahead of us in terms of academic integrity? As AI becomes better at writing with different voices at different levels for different audiences, AI detection will likely become even less effective than it currently is. Policies and practices should be adopted that embrace this reality.

There is so much to ponder about where AI should be used or controlled, and *many* lessons to learn from how social media, GPS, and the Internet of Things snuck into our lives. But like email and the internet, it is here, and it is going to become a part of modern life. You need to start playing and working with AI.

Key Themes

- AI is going to change working and thinking.
- AI is a new baseline for average or adequate.
- AI is a tool that can elevate the creativity and productivity of everyone.
- AI is only going to get better and more ubiquitous: specialized AI tools are about to proliferate.
- Faculty need to adapt with new policies, assignments, and assessments: AI detection will not be enough nor entirely dependable.
- All students will need AI literacy and will need to be able to use AI as a partner and collaborator.

AI offers a large set of new tools and capabilities, and curriculum and pedagogy will need updating. We will need new policies, support systems, classroom practices, grading rubrics, assignments, and assessment strategies, but faculty will need to understand the strengths and weakness of the variety of available AI and which tool to recommend for which task.

Students and parents already recognize that AI is an essential job skill: graduates who can think with AI to produce more, better, and faster results will be rewarded. An equity of outcomes demands that we equip all students for this new economy.

There will be new centers to train the next generation of AI programmers, but thinking and working with AI should be integrated into every part of the curriculum. Even more than digital literacy, AI literacy centers critical thinking: a complete education in the liberal arts has never mattered more.

Our curriculum and classrooms discussions also need immediately to include AI topics around ethics, data privacy, civics, environmental and energy costs, labor, discrimination, and bias. What are the potential unintended consequences for this new technology? How could it increase or decrease learning or justice? (Start with Benjamin, 2019; Heath & Segal, 2021; and The Civics of Technology Project.)

All of this new thinking will be done *with* AI. Education, parenting, and democracy have always managed an uneasy tension between what to think (content) and how to think (process). As the internet provided more immediate access to content, it profoundly shifted that balance to process. Our new future is teaching students how to think with AI.

A lot is at stake. In the summer of 2023, Gallup released a report that found perceptions of higher education continue to fall, even among college graduates—those who spent four years with us (Brenan, 2023). Could the revolution of AI be our opportunity to reflect and reimagine how we could most benefit our students, our society, our species, and our planet? This is a place where higher education can lead.

ACKNOWLEDGMENTS

Too many readers suffered through early drafts, but we are very grateful they did. The errors, absences, and mistakes remain ours alone, but it would have been much worse without the help and dedication of our diverse readers.

For the first couple of chapters, we needed real technical expertise as we tried to simplify a complex field. Edward A. Fox, Michael McCreary, Philip Gilks, and Alessandro Campioli all offered invaluable insight (often through multiple versions). The rest of the book (especially the difficult chapter on cheating) benefited from the insight of Michelle Denise Miller, Kate Drezek McConnell, Anna Mills, Rick Dakan, Sharon Valente, and Liam J. Watson. Many of them also provided tweaks to the assignments in the final chapters. Then we had our super-readers, who read virtually the entire book: Martin Sweidel, Kraig Robson, Bonni Stachowiak, and Stephanie Seketa.

All were motivated by the importance of this topic and their deep care for students. They helped us balance myriad difficult concerns, and their scholarship, insight, and kindness made this a much better book. Thank you.

We had lots of input from interviews with students (who mostly wanted to remain anonymous), but a few of them also volunteered to read sections of the book and agreed to be listed here. Thank you to Carter E. Watson and Noah Vetter for providing this essential perspective.

Thanks to the exceptionally profession team at Johns Hopkins University Press and especially to Greg Britton for this faith in this project, his constant encouragement, and his ability to move mountains and get this book through production at lightning speed. We're also thankful to the keen editorial eye of our copyeditor, Charles Dibble, who caught all the things we didn't, and Jessica Chittum, who ensured that our APA formatting was on point. A big cheer also to Ira Greenberg, whose AI images inspired several new assignments.

José also wishes to thank his wife Kimberly for her constant support and love: writing a book makes you weird, and she has now endured this process too many times (Maybe a few more?). The pets don't seem to mind, and he asks for forgiveness from all of those who got cat-caboose in Zoom meetings.

Eddie wishes to thank Liam and Carter for their reality checks and perspectives from the trenches. He also wishes to thank his wife, Joan, for talking about AI incessantly for the past few months and for sharing feedback and ideas throughout. I love you, home team! There's never a shortage of opinions about higher education in the Watson house.

REFERENCES

Abrams, Z. (2022). Student mental health is in crisis. Campuses are rethinking their approach. *American Psychological Association, Monitor on Psychology, 53*(7), Article 60. https://www.apa.org/monitor/2022/10/mental-health-campus-care

Acar, O. A. (2023, June 6). AI prompt engineering isn't the future. *Harvard Business Review*. https://hbr.org/2023/06/ai-prompt-engineering-isnt-the-future

Adlington A., & Eaton, S. E. (2021). *Contract cheating in Canada: Exploring legislative options* (Report No. 1880/114088). University of Calgary. https://dx.doi.org/10.11575/PRISM/39367

Al Kuwaiti, A., Nazer, K., Al-Reedy, A., Al-Shehri, S., Al Muhanna, A., Subbarayalu, A. V., Al Muhanna, D., & Al Muhanna, F. A. (2023). A review of the role of artificial intelligence in healthcare. *Journal of Personalized Medicine, 13*(6), Article 951. https://doi.org/10.3390/jpm13060951

American Association of Colleges and Universities. (2024a). *Essential learning outcomes*. https://www.aacu.org/trending-topics/essential-learning-outcomes

American Association of Colleges and Universities. (2024b). *VALUE rubrics*. https://www.aacu.org/initiatives/value-initiative/value-rubrics

American Association of Colleges and Universities. (2024c). *VALUE assignment design and diagnostic (ADD) tools*. https://www.aacu.org/initiatives/value-initiative/assignment-design-and-diagnostic-tool

American Association of Colleges and Universities. (2024d). *Integrative learning and signature work.* https://www.aacu.org/office-of-global-citizenship-for-campus-community-and-careers/integrative-learning

Anthropic. (2023, May 9). *Claude's constitution.* https://www.anthropic.com/index/claudes-constitution

Ardila, N. (2023, March 17). Artificial intelligence chatbots are slowly replacing human relationships. *Caplin News.* https://caplinnews.fiu.edu/artificial-intelligence-chatgpt-openai-loneliness-relationships/

Azerbayev, Z., Schoelkopf, H., Paster, K., Dos Santos, M., McAleer, S., Jiang, J. D., Biderman, S., & Welleck, S. (2023). *Llemma: An open language model for mathematics.* arXivLabs. https://doi.org/10.48550/arXiv.2310.10631

Bandura, A. (1997). *Self-efficacy: The exercise of control.* Freeman.

Bankhead, C. (2023, July 28). Hallucination, fake references: Cautionary tale about AI-generated abstracts. *MedPage Today.* https://www.medpagetoday.com/ophthalmology/generalophthalmology/105672

Bannon, M. T. (2023, June 22). How AI is changing the future of work. *Forbes.* https://www.forbes.com/sites/marenbannon/2023/06/22/how-ai-is-changing-the-future-of-work/?sh=

Barkley, E. F., Major, C. H, & Cross, K. P. (2014). *Collaborative learning techniques: A handbook for college faculty.* Jossey-Bass.

Beaty, R. E., & Johnson, D. R. (2021). Automating creativity assessment with SemDis: An open platform for computing semantic distance. *Behavior Research Methods, 53*, 757-780. https://doi.org/10.3758/s13428-020-01453-w

Benabou, R., & Tirole, J. (2003). Intrinsic and extrinsic motivation. *Review of Economic Studies, 70*(3), 489-520. http://dx.doi.org/10.1111/1467-937X.00253

Berman, H. M., Westbrook, J., Feng, Z., Gilliland, Z., Bhat, T. N., Weissig, H., Shindyalov, I. N., & Bourne, P. E. (2000). The protein data bank. *Nucleic Acids Research, 28*, 235-242. https://doi.org/10.1093/nar/28.1.235

Bernstein, A. (2023, May 23). *Master the art of prompt writing: 6 tips to writing better prompts* [Video]. YouTube. https://www.youtube.com/watch?v=cPf251bDKY0

Bharadwaj, P., Shaw, C., NeJame, L., Martin, S., Janson, N., & Fox, K. (2023). *Time for class 2023: Bridging student and faculty perspectives on*

digital learning. Tyton Partners. https://tytonpartners.com/time-for-class-2023/?utm_source=substack&utm_medium=email
Bodnick, M. (2023, July 18). ChatGPT goes to Harvard and does better than you think! *Slow Boring.* https://www.slowboring.com/p/chatgpt-goes-to-harvard?utm_source=substack&utm_medium=email
Bolger, K. (2023, September 28). How ChatGPT is putting college ghostwriters out of work. *The Walrus.* https://thewalrus.ca/chatgpt-ghost-writers/
Bonawitz, E., Shafto, P., Gweon, H., Goodman, N. D., Spelke, E., & Schulz, L. (2010). The double-edged sword of pedagogy: Instruction limits spontaneous exploration and discovery. *Cognition, 118*(3), 322-330. https://doi.org/10.1016/j.cognition.2010.10.001
Bond, J. (2023). *2022-2023 academic integrity report.* University of Maryland Division of Student Affairs, Office of Student Conduct. https://umd.app.box.com/s/r1q0ljkwoe7uho3rzvogt3zh9o4d7gdy
Bowen, J. A. (2006). Teaching naked: Why removing technology from your classroom will improve student learning. *National Forum for Teaching and Learning, 16*(1), 1-5. http://www.ntfl.com/
Bowen, J. A. (2011, December). *Beethoven the businessman* [Video]. TED Conferences. https://www.ted.com/talks/jose_bowen_beethoven_the_businessman
Bowen, J. A. (2012). *Teaching naked: How moving technology out of your college classroom will improve student learning.* Jossey-Bass.
Bowen, J. A. (2016). Building a socializing dorm to increase college student success. *Journal of College & University Student Housing, 43*(1), 28-39.
Bowen, J. A., & Watson, C. E. (2017). *Teaching naked techniques: A practical guide to designing better classes.* Jossey-Bass.
Bran, A. M., Cox, S., Schilter, O., Baldassari, C., White, A. D., & Schwaller, P. (2023). *ChemCrow: Augmenting large-language models with chemistry tools.* arXivLabs. https://doi.org/10.48550/arXiv.2304.05376
Brenan, M. (2023, July 11). Americans' confidence in higher education down sharply. *Gallup News.* https://news.gallup.com/poll/508352/americans-confidence-higher-education-down-sharply.aspx
Briggs, J., & Kodani, D. (2023). The potentially large effects of artificial intelligence on economic growth. *Goldman Sachs Global Economic Analyst Report.* https://www.gspublishing.com/content/research/en/reports/2023/03/27/d64e052b-0f6e-45d7-967b-d7be35fabd16.html

Brinkman, B. (2013). An analysis of student privacy rights in the use of plagiarism detection systems. *Science and Engineering Ethics, 19*, 1255-1266. https://doi.org/10.1007/s11948-012-9370-y

Brynjolfsson, E., Li, D., & Raymond, L. (2023). *Generative AI at work* (Working Paper No. w31161). National Bureau of Economic Research. https://doi.org/10.3386/w31161

Búi, C. (2023, September 21). Fueled in part by ChatGPT, academic integrity violations for 'unfair advantage' surge at Penn. *The Daily Pennsylvanian*. https://www.thedp.com/article/2023/09/penn-student-conduct-academic-integrity-cheating-plagiarism?utm_source=substack&utm_medium=email

Burrow, A. L., Hill, P. L., & Sumner, R. (2016). Leveling mountains: Purpose attenuates links between perceptions of effort and steepness. *Personality and Social Psychology Bulletin, 42*(1), 94-103. https://doi.org/10.1177%2F0146167215624196

Caulfield, J. (2023, June 2). Best AI detector: Free and premium tools compared. *Scribbr.* https://www.scribbr.com/ai-tools/best-ai-detector/

Chalmers, D. (2020, July 30). GPT-3 and general intelligence. *Daily Nous*. https://dailynous.com/2020/07/30/philosophers-gpt-3/#chalmers

Chechitelli, A. (2023, May 23). AI writing detection update from Turnitin's chief product officer. *TurnItIn.* https://www.turnitin.com/blog/ai-writing-detection-update-from-turnitins-chief-product-officer

Chegg. (2023). *Study tool.* https://www.chegg.com/study

Chen, T.-P. (2023, October 12). The annoying person in your work meeting might just be you. *The Wall Street Journal.* https://www.wsj.com/lifestyle/careers/ai-meetings-work-feedback-bots-bc380d72

Chen, Z., Qing, J., Xiang, T., Yue, W., & Zhou, J. (2022). *Seeing beyond the brain: Conditional diffusion model with sparse masked modeling for vision decoding.* arXivLabs. https://doi.org/10.48550/arXiv.2211.06956

Chickering, A., & Gamson, Z. (1987). Seven principles for good practice in undergraduate education. *AAHE Bulletin, March*, 3-7.

Choi, J. H., Hickman, K. E., Monahan, A., & Schwarcz, D. (2023, March 15). ChatGPT goes to law school. *Social Science Research Network.* http://dx.doi.org/10.2139/ssrn.4389233

Cline, S. (2023, July 20). How ChatGPT killed my discussion boards and prompted new prompts. *Times Higher Education/Inside Higher Education*. https://www.timeshighereducation.com/campus/how-chatgpt-killed-my-discussion-boards-and-prompted-new-prompts

Coffey, L. (2023a, August 4). Law schools split on ChatGPT in admissions essays. *Inside Higher Education*. https://www.insidehighered.com/news/tech-innovation/artificial-intelligence/2023/08/04/law-schools-split-using-chatgpt-admissions

Coffey, L. (2023b, November 14). AI voice clones and deepfakes: The latest presidents' engagement tools. *Inside Higher Education*. https://www.insidehighered.com/news/tech-innovation/artificial-intelligence/2023/11/14/presidents-use-ai-voice-clones-and

Conaway, J. K., & Wiesen, T. (2023). Academic dishonesty in online accounting assessments—Evidence on the use of academic resource sites. *Issues in Accounting Education, 38*(4), 45-60. https://doi.org/10.2308/ISSUES-2021-059

Cotton, D. R., Cotton, P. A., & Shipway, J. R. (2023). Chatting and cheating: Ensuring academic integrity in the era of ChatGPT. *Innovations in Education and Teaching International*, 1-12. https://doi.org/10.1080/14703297.2023.2190148

Covey, S. R. (2004). *The 7 habits of highly effective people: Restoring the character ethic* (Rev. ed.). Free Press.

Cummings, L. (2023). *AI syllabus language heuristic*. https://gamma.app/public/AI-Syllabus-Language-Heuristic-guqykesli4ekki5?mode=doc

Deci, E. L., & Ryan, R. M. (2000). The "what" and "why" of goal pursuits: Human needs and the self-determination of behavior. *Psychological Inquiry, 11*, 227-268. https://doi.org/10.1207/S15327965PLI1104_01

Desaire, H., Chua, A. E., Kim, M.-G., & Hua, D. (2023). Accurately detecting AI text when ChatGPT is told to write like a chemist. *Cell Reports Physical Science, 4*, Article 101672. https://doi.org/10.1016/j.xcrp.2023.101672

Dhandra, S. (2023, September 16). High school senior: Why aren't more teachers embracing AI? *CNN Opinion*. https://www.cnn.com/2023/09/16/opinions/ai-chatgpt-technology-chatbots-school-dhanda

Dreyfus, H. L. (1972). *What computers still can't do: A critique of artificial reason*. MIT Press.

Eaton, L. (2023). *Syllabi policies for AI generative tools*. https://docs.google.com/document/d/1RMVwzjc1o0Mi8Blw_-JUTcXv02b2WRH86vw7mi16W3U/edit

Eaton, S. E. (2021). *Plagiarism in higher education: Tackling tough topics in academic integrity*. Bloomsbury.

Eaton, S. E. (2023, February 24). 6 tenets of postplagiarism: Writing in the age of artificial intelligence. *Learning, Teaching and Leadership*. https://drsaraheaton.wordpress.com/2023/02/25/6-tenets-of-postplagiarism-writing-in-the-age-of-artificial-intelligence/

Eloundou, T., Manning, S., Mishkin, P., & Rock, D. (2023). *GPTs are GPTs: An early look at the labor market impact potential of large language models* (Working Paper No. 2303.10130). https://ideas.repec.org/p/arx/papers/2303.10130.html

Eyink, J. R., Motz, B. A., Heltzel, G., & Liddell, T. M. (2019). Student experiences with automated corrective feedback technology. *Journal of Applied Research in Higher Education, 11*(2), 326-342. https://doi.org/10.1108/JARHE-05-2018-0102

Fijačko, N., Gosak, L., Štiglic, G., Picard, C. T., & Douma, M. J. (2023). Can ChatGPT pass the life support exams without entering the American Heart Association course? *Resuscitation, 185*, Article 109732. https://doi.org/10.1016/j.resuscitation.2023.109732

Fyfe, P. (2022). How to cheat on your final paper: Assigning AI for student writing. *AI and Society, 38*, 1395-1405. https://doi.org/10.1007/s00146-022-01397-z

Gao, C. A., Howard, F. M., Markov, N. S., Dyer, E. C., Ramesh, S., Luo, Y., & Pearson, A. T. (2023). Comparing scientific abstracts generated by ChatGPT to real abstracts with detectors and blinded human reviewers. *npj Digital Medicine, 6*, Article 75. https://doi.org/10.1038/s41746-023-00819-6

Garst, K. (2023, July 27). Claude 2 vs GPT-4 in 2023: Comparing the top AI models. *LinkedIn*. https://www.linkedin.com/pulse/claude-2-vs-gpt-4-2023-comparing-top-ai-models-kim-garst/

Gee, J. P. (2005). *Why video games are good for your soul: Pleasure and learning*. Common Ground.

Geyer, A. (2023, March 13). GPT-4: What you need to know and what's different from GPT-3 and ChatGPT. *Ax Semantics*. https://en.ax-semantics.com/blog/gpt-4-and-whats-different-from-gpt-3

Ghaffary, S. (2023, September 21). Universities rethink using AI writing detectors to vet students' work. *Bloomberg.* https://www.bloomberg.com/news/newsletters/2023-09-21/universities-rethink-using-ai-writing-detectors-to-vet-students-work

Glass, A. L., & Kang, M. (2019). Fewer students benefit from doing homework than during the 1960s. *Phi Delta Kappan, 100*(7), 53-56. https://doi.org/10.1177%2F0031721719846889

Goel, A. K., & Polepeddi, L. (2016). *Jill Watson: A virtual teaching assistant for online education.* Georgia Institute of Technology. http://hdl.handle.net/1853/59104

Goebel, C. (2023, October 17). Are robots writing college essays? *Look at It This Way.* https://www.artsci.com/insights/strategic-insights-blog

Gorichanaz, T. (2023). Accused: How students respond to allegations of using ChatGPT on assessments. *Learning: Research and Practice, 9*(2), 183-196. https://doi.org/10.1080/23735082.2023.2254787

Grant, N., & Metz, C. (2022, June 12). Google sidelines engineer who claims its A.I. is sentient. *The New York Times.* https://www.nytimes.com/2022/06/12/technology/google-chatbot-ai-blake-lemoine.html

Greenberg, I. (2023). *Collections.* OBJKT. https://objkt.com/profile/tz1SmFz7vPbLaCR9fetjFuhHpqB4EUhX6wfd/collections

Griffith, E. (2023, March 16). GPT-4 vs. ChatGPT-3.5: What's the difference? *PC Magazine.* https://www.pcmag.com/news/the-new-chatgpt-what-you-get-with-gpt-4-vs-gpt-35

Grush, M., & Frydenberg, M. (2023, July 10). AI tools in education: Doing less while learning more. *CampusTechnology.* https://campustechnology.com/articles/2023/07/10/ai-tools-in-education-doing-less-while-learning-more.aspx?sra=ct_pulse_120723&oly_enc_id=3548G3906423B2X

Guar, A. (2023, November 27). UMD records at least 50 AI-related academic integrity cases in 2022-23. *The Diamondback.* https://dbknews.com/2023/11/27/umd-chatgpt-academic-integrity-cases/

Gupta, M. (2023, April 17). Harnessing the power of AI in the insurance sector. *Forbes.* https://www.forbes.com/sites/forbestechcouncil/2023/04/17/harnessing-the-power-of-ai-in-the-insurance-sector/?sh=13426d77335d

Hamid, R. D., & Schisgall, E. J. (2023, June 21). CS50 will integrate artificial intelligence into course instruction. *The Harvard Crimson.*

https://www.thecrimson.com/article/2023/6/21/cs50-artificial-intelligence/
Hassabis, D., Kumaran, D., & Maguire, E. A. (2007). Using imagination to understand the neural basis of episodic memory. *Journal of Neuroscience*, 27(52), 14365-14374. https://doi.org/10.1523/JNEUROSCI.4549-07.2007
Haverkamp, H. (2022, October 30). A teacher allows AI tools in exams—Here's what he learned. *The Decoder*. https://the-decoder.com/a-teacher-allows-ai-tools-in-exams-heres-what-he-learned/
Heath, M. K., & Segal, P. (2021). What pre-service teacher technology integration conceals and reveals: "Colorblind" technology in schools. *Computers & Education, 170,* Article 104225. https://doi.org/10.1016/j.compedu.2021.104225
Henderson, M. (2022, May 10). Radiology facing a global shortage. *Radiological Society of North America News*. https://www.rsna.org/news/2022/may/global-radiologist-shortage
Hines, K. (2023, July 12). Claude 2 offers 100k context windows and file uploads. *Search Engine Journal*. https://www.searchenginejournal.com/anthropic-launches-claude-2-with-100k-context-windows-file-uploads/491412/#close
Hoel, J. B., Parker, J., & Rivenburg, J. (2004). *Factors influencing persistence among nontraditional university students* (Working Paper No. 2004-001). SARUP Economics. https://mospace.umsystem.edu/xmlui/handle/10355/490
Hoover, A. (2023, August 17). Use of AI is seeping into academic journals—And it's proving difficult to detect. *Wired*. https://www.wired.com/story/use-of-ai-is-seeping-into-academic-journals-and-its-proving-difficult-to-detect/
Howard, J. (2023, February 21). Only 5.7% of US doctors are Black, and experts warn the shortage harms public health. *National Medical Association*. https://www.nmanet.org/news/632592/Only-5.7-of-US-doctors-are-Black-and-experts-warn-the-shortage-harms-public-health.htm
Hsu, S., Shah, R. S., Senthil, P., Ashktorab, Z., Dugan, C., Geyer, W., & Yang, D. (2023). *Helping the helper: Supporting peer counselors via AI-empowered practice and feedback*. arXivLabs. https://doi.org/10.48550/arXiv.2305.08982

Hu, K. (2023, February 2). ChatGPT sets record for fastest-growing user base—Analyst note. *Reuters.* https://www.reuters.com/technology/chatgpt-sets-record-fastest-growing-user-base-analyst-note-2023-02-01/

Hui, L., de Bruin, A. B. H., Donkers, J., & van Merriënboer, J. J. G. (2022). Why students do (or do not) choose retrieval practice: Their perceptions of mental effort during task performance matter. *Applied Cognitive Psychology, 36*(2), 433-444. https://doi.org/10.1002/acp.3933

Ibrahim, H., Asim, R., Zaffar, F., Rahwan, T., & Zaki, Y. (2023). Rethinking homework in the age of artificial intelligence. *IEEE Intelligent Systems, 38*, 24-27. http://dx.doi.org/10.1109/MIS.2023.3255599

Ibrahim, H., Liu, F., Asim, R., Battu, B., Benabderrahmane, S., Alhafni, B., Adnan, W., Alhanai, T., AlShebli, B., Baghdadi, R., Bélanger, J. J., Beretta, E., Celik, K., Chaqfeh, M., Daqaq, M. F., El Bernoussi, Z., Fougnie, D., de Soto, B. G., Gandolfi, A., . . . Zaki, Y. (2023). Perception, performance, and detectability of conversational artificial intelligence across 32 university courses. *Scientific Reports, 13*, Article 12187. https://doi.org/10.1038/s41598-023-38964-3

Intelligent.com. (2023, June 9). One-third of college students used ChatGPT for schoolwork during the 2022-23 academic year. *Intelligent.com.* https://www.intelligent.com/one-third-of-college-students-used-chatgpt-for-schoolwork-during-the-2022-23-academic-year/

Kahneman, D., Sibony, O., & Sunstein, C. R. (2021). *Noise: A flaw in human judgment.* Little, Brown Spark.

Kalliamvakou, E. (2022, September 7). Research: Quantifying GitHub Copilot's impact on developer productivity and happiness. *GitHub Blog.* https://github.blog/2022-09-07-research-quantifying-github-copilots-impact-on-developer-productivity-and-happiness/

Katz, D. M., Bommarito, M. J., Gao, S., & Arredondo, P. (2023, March 15). GPT-4 passes the bar exam. *Social Science Research Network.* http://dx.doi.org/10.2139/ssrn.4389233

Kirchner, J. H., Ahmad, L., Aaronson, S., & Leike, J. (2023, January 31). New AI classifier for indicating AI-written text. *OpenAI Blog.* https://openai.com/blog/new-ai-classifier-for-indicating-ai-written-text

Klein, E. (2023, July 11). A.I. could solve some of humanity's hardest problems. It already has: Demis Hassabis, the chief executive of

DeepMind, discusses how A.I. systems can accelerate scientific research [Audio podcast episode]. In *The Ezra Klein Show*. The New York Times. https://www.nytimes.com/2023/07/11/opinion/ezra-klein-podcast-demis-hassabis.html

Koivisto, M., & Grassini, S. (2023). Best humans still outperform artificial intelligence in a creative divergent thinking task. *Scientific Reports, 13*, Article 13601. https://doi.org/10.1038/s41598-023-40858-3

Korinek, A. (2023). *Language models and cognitive automation for economic research* (NBER Working Paper No. 30957). National Bureau of Economic Research. https://doi.org/10.3386/w30957

KP. (2023, September 13). People mocked me and said my essay-writing business was screwed when ChatGPT came out. So I fought like hell. *Insider*. https://www.businessinsider.com/essay-tutoring-writing-business-experience-chatgpt-2023-9

Krakauer, D. (2016, September 5). Will A.I. harm us? Better to ask how we'll reckon with our hybrid nature. *Nautilus*. https://nautil.us/will-ai-harm-us-better-to-ask-how-well-reckon-with-our-hybrid-nature-236098/

Kugel, S., & Hiltner, S. (2023, August 5). A new frontier for travel scammers: A.I.-generated guidebooks. *The New York Times*. https://www.nytimes.com/2023/08/05/travel/ai-travel-scams.html

Kumar, R. (2023). Faculty members' use of artificial intelligence to grade student papers: A case of implications. *International Journal for Educational Integrity, 19*(9), 1-10. https://doi.org/10.1007/s40979-023-00130-7

LaGorce, T. (2023, March 3). Need to write your vows? Chatbot wedding vows from ChatGPT and other AI. *The New York Times*. https://www.nytimes.com/2023/03/03/fashion/weddings/chatbot-wedding-vows-chatgpt-ai.html

Lång, K., Josefsson, V., Larsson, A. M., Larsson, S., Högberg, C., Sartor, H., Hofvind, S., Andersson, I., & Rosso, A. (2023). Artificial intelligence-supported screen reading versus standard double reading in the Mammography Screening with Artificial Intelligence trial (MASAI): A clinical safety analysis of a randomised, controlled, non-inferiority, single-blinded, screening accuracy study. *Lancet Oncology, 24*(8), 936-944. https://doi.org/10.1016/S1470-2045(23)00298-X

Langley, P. (2011). The changing science of machine learning. *Machine Learning, 82*(3), 275-279. https://doi.org/10.1007/s10994-011-5242-y

Li, D., Bledsoe, J. R., Zeng, Y., Liu, W., Hu, Y., Bi, K., Liang, A., & Li, S. (2020). A deep learning diagnostic platform for diffuse large B-cell lymphoma with high accuracy across multiple hospitals. *Nature Communications, 11*, Article 6004. https://doi.org/10.1038/s41467-020-19817-3

Liang, W., Yuksekgonul, M., Mao, Y., Wu, E., & Zou, J. (2023). GPT detectors are biased against non-native English writers. *Patterns, 6*, Article 100779. https://doi.org/10.1016/j.patter.2023.100779

Liu, Y., Mittal, A., Yang, D., & Bruckman, A. (2022). Will AI console me when I lose my pet? Understanding perceptions of AI-mediated email writing. *CHI '22: Proceedings of the 2022 CHI Conference on Human Factors in Computing Systems, USA,* Article 474. https://doi.org/10.1145/3491102.3517731

Lu, H., & Page, S. E. (2004). Groups of diverse problem solvers can outperform groups of high-ability problem solvers. *Proceedings of the National Academy of Sciences, USA, 101*(46), 16385-16389. https://doi.org/10.1073/pnas.0403723101

Lu, N., Liu, S., He, R., Wang, Q., & Tang, K. (2023). *Large language models can be guided to evade AI-generated text detection.* arXivLabs. https://doi.org/10.48550/arXiv.2305.10847

Makamson, K. (2023). *Stress testing claims with perplexity* [Image]. Department of Composition and Rhetoric, University of Mississippi

Martin, J. F., Jr. (2009). The goal of long division. *Teaching Children Mathematics, 15*(8), 482-487. https://www.jstor.org/stable/41199562

Maslej, N., Fattorini, L., Brynjolfsson, E., Etchemendy, J., Ligett, K., Lyons, T., Manyika, J., Ngo, H., Niebles, J. C., Parli, V., Shoham, Y., Wald, R., Clark, J., & Perrault, R. (2023). *The AI index 2023 annual report.* AI Index Steering Committee, Institute for Human-Centered AI, Stanford University. https://aiindex.stanford.edu/report/

Maynard, A. (2023, July 16). I asked ChatGPT to develop a college class about itself: Now, it's teaching it. *Slate.* https://slate.com/technology/2023/07/chatgpt-class-prompt-engineering.html

Mazur, E. (1996). *Peer instruction: A user's manual.* Prentice Hall.

McCabe, D. L., Butterfield, K. D., & Treviño, L. K. (2012). *Cheating in college: Why students do it and what educators can do about it.* Johns Hopkins University Press.

McKinsey & Company. (2023, August 1). *The state of AI in 2023: Generative AI's breakout year.* McKinsey Analytics. https://www

.mckinsey.com/capabilities/quantumblack/our-insights/the-state-of-ai-in-2023-generative-ais-breakout-year

Mills, A. (2022). *AI text generators and teaching writing: Starting points for inquiry* [White paper]. Middlebury College. https://sites.middlebury.edu/aiandwriting

Mills, A. (2023a). *A tale of two critiques.* AI Pedagogy Project, metaLAB at Harvard. https://aipedagogy.org/assignment/a-tale-of-two-critiques/

Mills, A. (2023b, March 23). ChatGPT just got better. What does that mean for our writing assignments? *Chronicle of Higher Education.* https://www.chronicle.com/article/chatgpt-just-got-better-what-does-that-mean-for-our-writing-assignments

Mnih, V., Kavukcuoglu, K., Silver, D., Graves, A., Antonoglou, I., Wierstra, D., & Riedmiller, M. (2015). Human-level control through deep reinforcement learning. *Nature, 518*(7540), 529-533. https://doi.org/10.1038/nature14236

Mollick, E. (2023, December 7). An opinionated guide to which AI to use: ChatGPT anniversary edition. *One Useful Thing.* https://www.oneusefulthing.org?utm_source=navbar&utm_medium=web&r=2kukct

Mollick, E. R., & Mollick, L. (2023a, March 7). Using AI to implement effective teaching strategies in classrooms: Five strategies, including prompts. *Social Science Research Network.* http://dx.doi.org/10.2139/ssrn.4391243

Mollick, E. R., & Mollick, L. (2023b, September 25). Student use cases for AI. *HBP Education.* https://hbsp.harvard.edu/inspiring-minds/student-use-cases-for-ai

Morrow, E., Zidaru, T., Ross, F., Mason, C., Patel, K. D., Ream, M., & Stockley, R. (2023). Artificial intelligence technologies and compassion in healthcare: A systematic scoping review. *Frontiers in Psychology, 13,* Article 971044. https://doi.org/10.3389/fpsyg.2022.971044

Moorthy, S., Pogacar, R., Khan, S., & Xu, Y. (2018). Is Nike female? Exploring the role of sound symbolism in predicting brand name gender. *Proceedings of the 2018 Conference on Empirical Methods in Natural Language Processing, USA,* 1128-1132. https://doi.org/10.18653/v1/D18-1142

The Museum of Modern Art. (2022). *Refik Anadol: Unsupervised machine hallucinations* [Exhibition]. https://www.moma.org/calendar/exhibitions/5535

National Association of Colleges and Employers (NACE). (2024). *What is career readiness?* https://www.naceweb.org/career-readiness/competencies/career-readiness-defined

Nettleton, J., & Ravinsky-Mayer, M. (2023). *FY 2023 annual disciplinary report for the University of Pennsylvania.* University of Pennsylvania Center for Community Standards and Accountability (CSA) and the Office of the Associate Vice President for Equity and Title IX. https://csa.upenn.edu/system/files/private-file-upload/2023/07/fy_2023_annual_disciplinary_report_final_draft.pdf

Newton, D. (2023). The cheat sheet. *Substack.* https://thecheatsheet.substack.com/

Newton, P. M. (2018). How common is commercial contract cheating in higher education and is it increasing? A systematic review. *Frontiers in Education, 3,* Article 67. https://doi.org/10.3389/feduc.2018.00067

Newton, P. M., & Essex, K. (2023). How common is cheating in online exams and did it increase during the COVID-19 pandemic? A systematic review. *Journal of Academic Ethics.* https://doi.org/10.1007/s10805-023-09485-5

Nicol, D. (2022). *Turning active learning into active feedback: Introductory guide.* Active Feedback Toolkit, Adam Smith Business School, University of Glasgow. https://doi.org/10.25416/NTR.19929290

Nicoletti, L., & Bass, D. (2023). Humans are biased: Generative AI is even worse. *Bloomberg Technology.* https://www.bloomberg.com/graphics/2023-generative-ai-bias/

Norman, D. A. (1991). Cognitive artifacts. In J. M. Carroll (Ed.), *Designing interaction: Psychology at the human-computer interface* (pp. 17-38). Cambridge University Press.

Noy, S., & Zhang, W. (2023). Experimental evidence on the productivity effects of generative artificial intelligence. *Science, 381*(6614), 187-192. https://doi.org/10.1126/science.adh2586

OpenAI. (2022, November 30). Introducing ChatGPT research assistant! *OpenAI Blog.* https://openai.com/blog/chatgpt/

Oregon State University (OSU) Ecampus. (2023). *Bloom's taxonomy revisited.* https://ecampus.oregonstate.edu/faculty/artificial-intelligence-tools/blooms-taxonomy-revisited.pdf

Ott, M. (2023, May 2). Chegg's stock plunges on fears of competition from ChatGPT. *AP News.* https://apnews.com/article/chegg-stock-shares-chatgpt-ai-a877423bd4a8f67b1494363fc81cf52a

Owens, H. (2015). Cheating within online assessments: A comparison of cheating behaviors in proctored and unproctored environment (Publication No. 19704) [Doctoral dissertation]. Mississippi State University Scholars Junction. https://scholarsjunction.msstate.edu/td/1049/

Pak, J. (2023, August 21). Chinese animation house puts AI capabilities to the test. *Marketplace.* https://www.marketplace.org/2023/08/21/generative-ai-animation-production-china/

Paris, F., & Buchanan, L. (2023, April 14). 35 ways real people are using A.I. right now. *The New York Times.* https://www.nytimes.com/interactive/2023/04/14/upshot/up-ai-uses.html

Pavlik, J. V. (2023). Collaborating with ChatGPT: Considering the implications of generative artificial intelligence for journalism and media education. *Journalism and Mass Communication Educator, 78*(1), 84-93. https://doi.org/10.1177/10776958223223607

Pep Talk Radio. (2023). In-depth review of Claude 2: The conversational AI assistant [Audio podcast episode]. In *Pep Talk Radio.* https://www.peptalkradio.com/in-depth-review-of-claude-2/

Perez, S. (2023, November 3). Apple CEO Tim Cook says AI is a fundamental technology, confirms investments in generative AI. *TechCrunch+.* https://techcrunch.com/2023/11/03/apple-ceo-tim-cook-says-ai-is-a-fundamental-technology-confirms-investments-in-generative-ai/

Perkins, M., Roe, J., Postma, D., McGaughran, J., & Hickerson, D. (2023). Detection of GPT-4 generated text in higher education: Combining academic judgement and software to identify generative AI tool misuse. *Journal of Academic Ethics.* https://doi.org/10.1007/s10805-023-09492-6

Plagiarism Checker. (2021, July 23). 5 reasons why all students should use a plagiarism checker. *Plagiarism Checker Articles.* https://www.plagiarismchecker.net/dev/5-reasons-plagiarism-checker/

Prabhu, A. (2023, August 21). London's YouMakr.ai raises $500K for AI tool predicting exam questions. *TechFundingNews*. https://techfundingnews.com/londons-youmakr-ai-raises-500k-for-ai-tool-predicting-exam-questions/#google_vignette

Purdue University Department of Computer Science. (2023). *Artificial intelligence degree requirements*. https://www.cs.purdue.edu/undergraduate/curriculum/bachelor-ai.html

Quizlet. (2023, June 24). Quizlet's state of AI in education survey reveals teachers are surprise AI champions. *Cision PR Newswire*. https://www.prnewswire.com/news-releases/quizlets-state-of-ai-in-education-survey-reveals-teachers-are-surprise-ai-champions-301884427.html

Rattner, S. (2023, July 10). Full speed ahead on A.I. Our economy needs it. *The New York Times*. https://www.nytimes.com/2023/07/10/opinion/ai-economy-productivity-jobs-workers.html

Rho, E. H., Harrington, M., Zhong, Y., & Eberhardt, J. L. (2023). Escalated police stops of Black men are linguistically and psychologically distinct in their earliest moments. *Proceedings of the National Academy of Sciences, USA, 120*(23), e2216162120. https://doi.org/10.1073/pnas.2216162120

Rock, D., & Grant, H. (2016, November 4). Why diverse teams are smarter. *Harvard Business Review*. https://hbr.org/2016/11/why-diverse-teams-are-smarter

Rodriques, S. (2023, November 1). *Announcing Future House* [Press release]. FutureHouse. https://www.futurehouse.org/articles/announcing-future-house

Rose, K. (2023, July 11). Inside the white-hot center of A.I. doomerism. *The New York Times*. https://www.nytimes.com/2023/07/11/technology/anthropic-ai-claude-chatbot.html

Russell Group. (2023, July 4). *Russell Group principles on the use of generative AI tools in education*. https://russellgroup.ac.uk/media/6137/rg_ai_principles-final.pdf

Sadasivan, V. S., Kumar, A., Balasubramanian, S., Wang, W., & Feizi, S. (2023). *Can AI-generated text be reliably detected?* arXivLabs. https://doi.org/10.48550/arXiv.2303.11156

Samuel, A. L. (1959). Some studies in machine learning using the game of checkers. *IBM Journal of Research and Development, 3*(3), 210-229. https://doi.org/10.1147/rd.33.0210

Sayers, D. (2023, May 25). A simple hack to ChatGPT-proof assignments using Google Drive. *Times Higher Education*. https://www.timeshighereducation.com/campus/simple-hack-chatgptproof-assignments-using-google-drive

Schade, M. (2023). Fine-tuning a classifier to improve truthfulness. *OpenAI*. https://help.openai.com/en/articles/5528730-fine-tuning-a-classifier-to-improve-truthfulness

Schmieden, K. (2019, July 24). Feeling in control: Bank of America helps customers to "keep the change." *This Is Design Thinking*. https://thisisdesignthinking.net/2018/09/feeling-in-control-bank-of-america-helps-customers-to-keep-the-change/

Science News Staff. (2007, December 21). The runners-up. *Science, 318*(5858), 1844-1849. https://doi.org/10.1126/science.318.5858.1844a

Shaikh, E. (2023, July 29). ChatGPT vs Claude 2: A detailed analysis (Expert view). *Demand Sage*. https://www.demandsage.com/chatgpt-vs-claude/

Sharma, A., Lin, I. W., Miner, A. S., Atkins, D. C., & Althoff, T. (2023) Human–AI collaboration enables more empathic conversations in text-based peer-to-peer mental health support. *Nature Machine Intelligence, 5*, 46-57. https://doi.org/10.1038/s42256-022-00593-2

Shaw, C., Yuan, L., Brennan, D., Martin, S., Janson, N., Fox, K., & Bryant, G. (2023, October 23). *Tyton Partners*. https://tytonpartners.com/time-for-class-2023/genai-update

Shoshan, Y., Bakalo, R., Gilboa-Solomon, F., Ratner, V., Barkan, E., Ozery-Flato, M., Amit, M., Khapun, D., Ambinder, E. B., Oluyemi, E. T., Panigrahi, B., DiCarlo, P. A., Rosen-Zvi, M., & Mullen, L. A. (2022). Artificial intelligence for reducing workload in breast cancer screening with digital breast tomosynthesis. *Radiology, 303*(1), 69-77. https://doi.org/10.1148/radiol.211105

Simonite, T. (2015, February 25). Google's AI masters space invaders (But it still stinks at Pac-Man). *MIT Technology Review*. https://www.technologyreview.com/2015/02/25/73349/googles-ai-masters-space-invaders-but-it-still-stinks-at-pac-man

Simonite, T. (2016, March 31). How Google plans to solve artificial intelligence. *MIT Technology Review*. https://www.technologyreview.com/2016/03/31/161234/how-google-plans-to-solve-artificial-intelligence

Simonton, D. K. (1997). Creative productivity: A predictive and explanatory model of career trajectories and landmarks. *Psychological Review, 104*(1), 66-89. https://doi.org/10.1037/0033-295X.104.1.66

Sjoquist, D. L., & Winters, J. V. (2012). State merit-based financial aid programs and college attainment. *Journal of Regional Science, 55*(3), 364-390. https://doi.org/10.1111/jors.12161

Steipe, B. (2022, December 29). Just the principles . . . Three principles for AI in the academy. *Sentient Syllabus.* https://sentientsyllabus.substack.com/p/just-the-basics

Stearns, S. A. (2001). The student-instructor relationship's effect on academic integrity. *Ethics and Behavior, 11*(3), 275-285. https://doi.org/10.1207/S15327019EB1103_6

Stoner, J. (2023, March 22). What is Moore's law and how does it impact AI? *Unite.AI.* https://www.unite.ai/moores-law/

Student Voice. (2021). *Prioritizing academic integrity among students.* College Pulse. https://reports.collegepulse.com/student-voice-academic-integrity

Study.com. (2023). *Productive teaching tool or innovative cheating?* https://study.com/resources/perceptions-of-chatgpt-in-schools

Sung, G., Guillain, L., & Schneider, B. (2023). Can AI help teachers write higher quality feedback? Lessons learned from using the GPT-3 engine in a makerspace course. In P. Blikstein, J. Van Aalst, R. Kizito, & K. Brennan, K. (Eds.), *Proceedings of the 17th International Conference of the Learning Sciences* (pp. 2093-2094). International Society of the Learning Sciences. https://repository.isls.org//handle/1/10177

Suri, A., Tang, S., Kargilis, D., Taratuta, E., Kneeland, B. J., Choi, G., Agarwal, A., Anabaraonye, N., Xu, W., Parente, J. B., Terry, A., Kalluri, A., Song, K., & Rajapakse, C. S. (2023). Conquering the Cobb angle: A deep learning algorithm for automated, hardware-invariant measurement of Cobb angle on radiographs in patients with scoliosis. *Radiology: Artificial Intelligence, 5*(4). https://doi.org/10.1148/ryai.220158

Swaak, T. (2023, September 27). 'We're all using it': Publishing decisions are increasingly aided by AI. That's not always obvious. *The Chronicle of Higher Education.* https://www.chronicle.com/article/were-all-using-it-publishing-decisions-are-increasingly-aided-by-ai-thats-not-always-obvious

Takagi, Y., & Nishimoto, S. (2023, March 11). High-resolution image reconstruction with latent diffusion models from human brain activity. *BioRxiv.* https://doi.org/10.1101/2022.11.18.517004

Teja, R. (2023, September 5). I made a video game using ChatGPT! My journey in developing an Android game from scratch. *Medium.* https://levelup.gitconnected.com/i-made-a-video-game-using-chatgpt-9b0c03fcdcbe

Terry, O. K. (2023, May 12). I'm a student. You have no idea how much we're using ChatGPT. No professor or software could ever pick up on it. *The Chronicle of Higher Education.* https://www.chronicle.com/article/im-a-student-you-have-no-idea-how-much-were-using-chatgpt

Thier, J. (2023, March 9). New AI jobs: Someone with a 'hacker spirit' can earn over $300,000 for a new kind of job centered around ChatGPT-like assistants. *Fortune.* https://fortune.com/2023/03/09/new-ai-jobs-chatgpt-like-assistants

Thunström, A. O. (2022, June 30). We asked GPT-3 to write an academic paper about itself—Then we tried to get it published. *Scientific American.* https://www.scientificamerican.com/article/we-asked-gpt-3-to-write-an-academic-paper-about-itself-mdash-then-we-tried-to-get-it-published

Tunyasuvunakool, K., Adler, J., Wu, Z., Green, T., Zielinski, M., Žídek, A., Bridgland, A., Cowie, A., Meyer, C., Laydon, A., Velankar, S., Kleywegt, G. J., Bateman, A., Evans, R., Pritzel, A., Figurnov, M., Ronneberger, O., Bates, R., Kohl, S. A. A., . . . Hassabis, D. (2021). Highly accurate protein structure prediction for the human proteome. *Nature, 596,* 590-596. https://doi.org/10.1038/s41586-021-03828-1

Turing, A. M. (1950). Computing machinery and intelligence. *Mind, 49,* 433-460. https://doi.org/10.1093/mind/LIX.236.433

Turnitin. (2023, July 25). *Turnitin AI detection feature reviews more than 65 million papers* [Press release]. Cision PR Newswire. https://www.prnewswire.com/news-releases/turnitin-ai-detection-feature-reviews-more-than-65-million-papers-301885203.html

Tversky, A., & Kahneman, D. (1974). Judgment under uncertainty: Heuristics and biases. *Science, 185*(4157), 1124-1131. https://www.jstor.org/stable/1738360

Uszkoreit, J. (2017, August 31). Transformer: A novel neural network architecture for language understanding. *Google Research Blog.* https://blog.research.google/2017/08/transformer-novel-neural-network.html

Utley, J., & Klebahn, P. (2022). *Ideaflow: The only business metric that matters.* Penguin.

Vahid, F., Downey, K., Pang, A., & Gordon, C. (2023). Impact of several low-effort cheating-reduction methods in a CS1 class. *Proceedings of the 2023 ACM SIGCSE Technical Symposium on Computer Science Education, USA,* 486-492. https://doi.org/10.1145/3545945.3569731

Vaswani, A., Shazeer, N., Parmar, N., Uszkoreit, J., Jones, L., Gomez, A. N., Kaiser, Ł., & Polosukhin, I. (2017). Attention is all you need. In I. Guyon, U. Von Luxburg, S. Bengio, H. Wallach, R. Fergus, S. Vishwanathan, & R. Garnett, *Advances in neural information processing systems 30.* https://papers.nips.cc/paper_files/paper/2017/hash/3f5ee243547dee91fbd053c1c4a845aa-Abstract.html

Vygotsky, L. S. (1978). *Mind in society: The development of higher psychological processes.* Harvard University Press.

Waldfogel, J. (2009). *Scroogenomics: Why you shouldn't buy presents for the holidays.* Princeton University Press.

Watson, J. (2023, March 6). Computer science researchers lead the defense against the dark side of tech. *Virginia Tech Daily.* https://vtnews.vt.edu/articles/2023/02/eng-cs-deepfake-research-bimal-viswanath.html

Walton Family Foundation. (2023). *Teachers and parents report positive impact of ChatGPT on teaching and learning.* Impact Research. https://www.waltonfamilyfoundation.org/learning/teachers-parents-report-positive-impact-of-chatgpt-on-teaching-and-learning

Weber-Wulff, D., Anohina-Naumeca, A., Bjelobaba, S., Foltýnek, T., Guerrero-Dib, J., Popoola, O., Šigut, P., & Waddington, L. (2023). *Testing of detection tools for AI-generated text.* arXivLabs. https://doi.org/10.48550/arXiv.2306.15666

Weilding, L. (2023, March 27). Half of college students say using AI on schoolwork is cheating or plagiarism. *Best Colleges.* https://www.bestcolleges.com/research/college-students-ai-tools-survey/

Weinberg, B. A., & Galenson, D. W. (2019). Creative careers: The life cycles of Nobel laureates in economics. *De Economist, 167,* 221-239. https://doi.org/10.1007/s10645-019-09339-9

White, S. K. (2023, October 13). 11 most in-demand gen AI jobs companies are hiring for. *CIO.* https://www.cio.com/article/655291/most-in-demand-generative-ai-jobs.html

Whiting, K. (2023, March 2). 3 new and emerging jobs you can get hired for this year. *World Economic Forum.* https://www.weforum.org/agenda/2023/03/new-emerging-jobs-work-skills

Whitten, A. (2023, July). Me, myself, and AI: Artificial intelligence has entered a new era. Here's how we stay human. *Stanford Magazine.* https://stanfordmag.org/contents/me-myself-and-ai

Wiley. (2023). *Higher ed's next chapter, 2023-2024: Four trends reshaping the learning landscape.* https://www.wiley.com/en-us/network/trending-stories/trends-in-higher-education-2023-2024-shaping-the-learning-landscape

Wilson, E. O. (2017). *The origins of creativity.* Liveright.

Yan-Ran, W., Qu, L., Sheybani, N. D., Luo, X., Wang, J., Hawk, K. E., Theruvath, A. J., Gatidis, S., Xiao, X., Pribnow, A., Rubin, D., & Daldrup-Link, H. E. (2023). AI transformers for radiation dose reduction in serial whole-body PET scans. *Radiology: Artificial Intelligence, 5*(3). https://doi.org/10.1148/ryai.220246

Yang, C., Wang, X., Lu, Y., Liu, H., Le, Q. V., Zhou, D., & Chen X. (2023). *Large language models as optimizers.* arXivLabs. https://doi.org/10.48550/arXiv.2309.03409

Young, J. R. (2018, April 13). Can a 'family of bots' reshape college teaching? *EdSurge.* https://www.edsurge.com/news/2018-04-13-can-a-family-of-bots-reshape-college-teaching

Yu, H., Marschke, G., Ross, M. B., Staudt, J., & Weinberg. B. (2023). Publish or perish: Selective attrition as a unifying explanation for patterns in innovation over the career. *Journal of Human Resources, 58*(4) 1307-1346. https://doi.org/10.3368/jhr.59.2.1219-10630R1

Zaromb, F. M., & Roediger, H. L. (2010). The testing effect in free recall is associated with enhanced organizational processes. *Memory & Cognition, 38*(8), 995-1008. https://doi.org/10.3758/MC.38.8.995

Zimmerman, J. (2023, August 29). Here's my AI policy for students: I don't have one. *The Washington Post.* https://www.washingtonpost.com/opinions/2023/08/29/ai-student-policy-chatgpt-college/

INDEX

The American Association of Colleges and Universities (AAC&U) is a global membership organization dedicated to advancing the democratic purposes of higher education by promoting equity, innovation, and excellence in liberal education. Through our programs and events, publications and research, public advocacy, and campus-based projects, AAC&U serves as a catalyst and facilitator for innovations that improve educational quality and equity and that support the success of all students. In addition to accredited public and private, two-year, and four-year colleges and universities and state higher education systems and agencies throughout the United States, our membership includes degree-granting higher education institutions in more than twenty-five countries as well as other organizations and individuals.

Visit: aacu.org

@aacu **/AACandU** **/company/aacu**